Canyon Country Hiking

and Natural History

A hiking guide
to southeastern Utah with a description
of the natural history of the area

By

F. A. Barnes

Wasatch Publishers, Inc.

Published by
Wasatch Publishers, Inc.
4647 Idlewild Road
Salt Lake City, Utah 84117
© Copyright 1977 by Wasatch Publishers, Inc.
All Rights Reserved

Third Printing 1981

All photographs and maps by the
author except as otherwise noted.

Library of Congress Catalog No. 76-58119
I.S.B.N. o-915272-07-5

Contents

TRAIL DESCRIPTIONS

3

SHORT HIKING TALES

Acknowledgments

I want to express my sincere thanks to the many people who have aided me with their detailed personal knowledge about certain areas. These were primarily certain employees of the three federal agencies which administer most of canyon country, the U.S. Forest Service, the National Park Service and the Bureau of Land Management. In most cases their helpfulness went far beyond the call of duty.

I also wish publicly to express my deepest appreciation for the help I have received in the many aspects of preparing this book from my secretary, camera grip, typist, grammarian, proofreader, photo model and faithful fellow hiker, all of whom are the same person—my wife of over a quarter century. May our next quarter century together be as happy, adventurous and rewarding. And may those who read and use this book be inspired to seek out and explore the places described, and thus come to know and love the canyon country of southeastern Utah as we do.

Fran Barnes

6

Biographical Sketch of the Author

In the mid 1960s, Fran Barnes gave up a long and successful career as a west coast aerospace engineer to "follow the seasons" with his wife and young daughter in a big travel trailer. On top of the truck that towed the trailer a powerboat rode on a rig Fran designed and built. Inside the truck were two trail cycles and an assortment of recreation gear.

The Barnes family lived and traveled in this rig for a total of four years, year around, following a seasonal route that put them in the Sierra foothills in the spring, north via the western mountain ranges and into the Canadian Rockies in the summer, then south to spend autumn enjoying the desert lakes of Nevada and Arizona before heading for winter quarters on the west coast of Mexico.

As they followed this leisurely, seasonal travel route, the Barneses stopped for weeks, and even months, at the most

Photo by Terby Barnes

primitive and beautiful areas of the western states that they could find, pursuing their varied outdoor studies and recreational interests. They enjoyed and became proficient at waterskiing, hiking, trail cycling, skindiving and backcountry exploring by several means.

While they traveled, Fran added to his already huge collection of scenic, recreational and nature photographs and wrote articles for travel-oriented magazines, thus turning his engineering writing experience and photography hobby into a new career.

Fran's first travel article was published in *Trailer Life* magazine as a cover feature in 1966. Since then, he has sold several hundred travel and outdoor recreation articles to a wide variety of magazines, news papers and other publications, illustrating them with his own photographs and other graphics. He has also published several of his own travel guides.

On one of their seasonal swings south, the Barneses "discovered" the canyon country of southeastern Utah. In 1969, after a third lengthy visit, they decided to stay there. Since then, Mrs. Barnes—Terby to her many friends—has made a new career with the National Park Service, and their daughter, Terry, has entered a Utah university in search of an outdoor-oriented education.

From his Moab base, Fran has pursued his new writing and photography profession with vigor and effectiveness, specializing in many aspects of the unique Four Corners region known as the Colorado Plateau.

In preparing this book, Fran has drawn upon 12 years of experience at exploring the unique canyon country of Utah by every means available—by automobile and light airplane; by powerboat, houseboat, rubber raft and canoe; by trail cycle, sandbuggy, four wheel drive and snowmobile; and—last but not least—on foot, following trails where they exist, but mostly finding his own way through wild country seldom seen by anyone.

From this experience, Fran offers hikers not only a listing of all established trails within his favorite region of canyon country, but also several approaches to exploring this fantastically different land where trails do not exist.

Mel Davis, Publisher

Introduction

Region Covered

"Canyon country" is essentially the southeastern corner of Utah, where the Colorado River and its numerous tributaries have carved a veritable maze of deep canyons into Cretaceous, Jurassic, Triassic, Permian and Pennsylvanian rock strata. The term "canyonlands" is also applied to this region by those who live there, but since this word was used in the naming of Canyonlands National Park, most people now associate "canyonlands" with just the park. Hence the use of the more general term "canyon country" in this book.

Geographically and geologically, canyon country encompasses almost the entire southeastern half of Utah. For practical purposes, however, half of a state is too large an area to cover in one hiking book.

Thus, this volume is limited to just that part of Utah that is bounded by the Green and Colorado rivers on the west, Interstate 70 on the north, the Navajo Indian Reservation boundary on the south and the Colorado-Utah border on the east.

There is more than enough unusual and challenging hiking within just that region to keep a very active and dedicated hiker going for years.

General Terrain

Most of the canyon country covered by this book is classified as "high desert," but within this region two mountain ranges soar upward above the desert to alpine heights. Elevations range from slightly below 4000 feet in the Colorado River gorge to almost 13,000 feet in the mountains.

While the region is high desert in general, that term hardly describes this unique land. Four major rivers, the Green, Colorado, San Juan and Dolores, slash deeply into ancient igneous, sedimentary and aeolian rock, creating magnificent, sheer-walled gorges. Literally

9

thousands of lesser canyons branch and rebranch in labyrinthine complexity from these river gorges. Most of these side canyons are dry except for occasional springs, but some have enough water to provide intermittent, seasonal flow. A few contain perennial streams.

These canyons and gorges break up the high desert into broad "sand flats," isolated mesas, high buttes and jutting peninsulas. These, in turn, are further jumbled by massive distortions in the earth's crust in many places, by immense rock outcroppings and by a series of strange "salt valleys." The town of Moab lies in one such valley, which has the peculiar characteristic of being high at both ends. The Colorado River enters and leaves this deep valley through "portals" in the sheer cliffs that wall the valley.

Two mountain ranges soar high above all other geologic features in the region. The La Sals lie to the southeast of Moab, and the Abajos are to the west and north of Monticello and Blanding. Both of these fairly small, isolated ranges are the unique "laccolithic" mountains that occur only in the Four Corners area of this nation. The novel way in which these ranges formed left them with highly unusual "foothills." These "foothills" for both ranges are a series of deep, spectacular redrock canyons separated by high, sloping mesas. The foothill canyons, especially those radiating in all directions from the Abajos, were once occupied by the prehistoric Anasazi Indians. The La Sal foothill canyons show only traces of Anasazi use, most of it related to hunting and foraging, with few signs of permanent habitation.

The canyon country of southeastern Utah is the product of relatively recent geologic activity. Some Four Corners laccolithic mountains and many other major features formed during the Laramide orogeny 50 to 75 million years ago when the whole region was convulsed by violent crustal activity. Current scientific theory holds that the La Sal, Henry and Abajo laccolithic ranges formed somewhat more recently. Then, about 10 million years ago, the entire region was uplifted 4000 to 6000 feet, drastically accelerating water run-off. This led to the spectacular erosional forms—the canyons, cliffs, buttes, spires, mountains and mesas—that give the canyon country of southeastern Utah its unique beauty.

Land Administration

In most of this country, hikers who do not confine themselves to a few established trails soon find their explorations cut short by fences, freeways and privately owned land. This is not true in Utah, where seventy-five percent of the state's area is under federal administration. In canyon country the figure is over ninety percent.

From this enormously administered area, some is set aside as Indian reservation, but most is public land administered variously by the National Park Service, National Forest Service or Bureau of Land Management. With few restrictions, all land under these agencies is open to hiking.

10

In canyon country, private and state land is rare with most of it being around the few towns, in agricultural areas to the east and north of Monticello, and in a few scattered locations in the mountains. There are, of course, quite a number of patented mining claims here and there which are also private property, but these are always small in area. Most of the few isolated ranches were originally claimed under federal homestead laws or purchased directly from the BLM. Some were established before Utah became a state.

There are fences in canyon country, but most of these either mark boundaries, such as National Forests, or have been erected on public land to restrict the movement of grazing sheep and cattle. Gates through such fences are never locked, but if opened should be carefully closed. The fences and gates are there to control domestic livestock, not people. This is true even with some private land in the mountains, unless otherwise posted, especially where public roads cross private land.

Because of the wild, rugged and remote nature of canyon country, it is wise for long-range hikers to register first with one or more of the appropriate federal land administration offices. These are located in the major towns and at the National Parks and Monuments. The National Park Service has a back-country permit system that is applicable to Arches and Canyonlands National Park and Natural Bridges National Monument.

Antiquities Laws

There are both state and federal laws protecting all antiquities on public land in Utah, including prehistoric Indian structures and artifacts, historic sites and artifacts, fossilized wood and bone, and items of scientific interest.

The Federal Act for the Preservation of American Antiquities, June 8, 1906, says in part that, without a special permit that is granted only to qualified scientific or educational institutions, it is unlawful to "...appropriate, excavate, injure or destroy any historic or prehistoric ruin or monument, or any object of antiquity..." or "other objects of historic or scientific interest that are situated upon lands owned or controlled by" the federal government.

Utah State has a similar law protecting antiquities within its borders that are not on federal land, but may also be applied to federal land in some cases.

Canyon country is rich in all kinds of fascinating and scientifically valuable objects of antiquity. Alert hikers may even make original discoveries, but the laws require that such discoveries on public land be reported to the appropriate land administration agency. Amateur collectors may take certain types of specimens from public land, such as sea-life fossils, gemstones and small amounts of petrified wood, but collecting even these for resale is prohibited except by special permit.

Collecting petrified bone in any amount is not allowed, and collecting of any sort is prohibited in national parks and monuments. Glen Canyon National Recreation Area, part of which is within the region covered by this book, has its own regulations governing the collection of specimens. For details, write Superintendent, Glen Canyon National Recreation Area, Box 1507, Page, AZ 86040.

Discoveries of antiquities or other objects of scientific or historical value should be reported to the appropriate land administration agencies. Within the region covered by this book, the Bureau of Land Management and Forest Service maintain offices in Moab and Monticello. The National Park Service has offices in Moab, Monticello, Arches National Park, Natural Bridges National Monument, at the three entrances to Canyonlands National Park, and at the Hite and Hall's Crossing visitor areas on upper Lake Powell. The Utah State Department of Forestry, which administers part of the eastern slopes of the La Sal Mountains, has an office in Moab. Discoveries made on other state land should be reported to the appropriate departments at any of the major universities in Utah.

Seasonal Variations

The climate in canyon country varies from arid to semi-arid in the lower elevations, with heavier precipitation in the mountains, depending upon elevation and other variables.

The entire region has four definite seasons, although at times it may seem that spring and winter have been transposed.

SPRING weather can be quite variable. In canyon country, spring comes early, in late February or early March, but often demonstrates more weather instability than winter. Winds are common, some precipitation falls; snow above 5000 feet, rain below that level. Cloudiness and overcast from passing storm systems are common, even though many drop little or no precipitation on the lower elevations of canyon country. Despite all this, perhaps fifty percent of the spring days are beautiful, with clear to lightly clouded skies, light breezes or none at all and temperatures in the 60s and 70s. Nights are generally cool, in the 20s and 30s in early spring, the 40s and 50s later.

SUMMER in canyon country, by some standards, starts early, in May or even earlier some years. The warmest time of the summer is, with few exceptions, between mid-June and mid-August. Then, daytime maximums in the lower elevations will vary between 90 and 100 degrees. Higher temperatures are rare and generally of brief duration. During this period, nights are still cool enough for comfortable sleeping, generally in the 60s or 70s. Before mid-June there may be warm days, but rarely above 95 degrees and then only for a day or so. In mid-August, the heat usually breaks because a stormy season sets in about that time. This generally takes the form of scattered and brief thundershowers. Such storms, in whatever season they hit, are almost always accompanied by strong winds. In canyon country, summer heat is always accompanied by low humidity, making it subjectively more bearable than much lower temperatures with high humidity.

AUTUMN in canyon country is long and beautiful, with warm, clear, windless days in the 50s, 60s and 70s, and nights 20 to 30 degrees cooler, from mid-September through mid-November and sometimes even later. Some years even December enjoys Indian Summer weather. Autumn sometimes has short storms and even brief hot spells, but for the most part has the most reliably delightful weather of the year.

WINTER in canyon country is generally calm, clear and with daytime temperatures in the 20s, 30s and 40s in lower elevations, getting colder with each gain in elevation. Below-zero temperatures, even at night, are rare at lower elevations. The winter calm is broken occasionally by passing storm systems, which usually leave new snow above 5000 feet, occasionally at all elevations. In general, winter in canyon country begins in mid-November as far as temperatures are concerned, but the first snow, except in the high mountains, may not fall until late December. The La Sal and Abajo mountains usually have snow on their upper elevations from late October through early May, or even later if the winter snows were heavy. The mid-elevations, from 5000 to 7000 feet, generally have some snow each winter, but it is lighter and does not last as long. Below 5000 feet, some snow may be deposited by large storms, but it rarely lasts more than a few days except on slopes that are protected from the sun.

In general, the mountain ranges of canyon country have the same weather as other western ranges. From late spring through early fall, rain is fairly frequent. For the rest of the year, precipitation takes the form of snow. Temperatures seldom exceed 80 degrees even in midsummer.

In sum, normal canyon country weather permits hiking year around at most or all elevations, with the exception being the higher mountain areas in the winter. Even there, however, there are hikers who enjoy snow-shoeing or cross-country skiing through the frigid beauty of a mountain winter. Winters too severe to permit ordinary hiking below 6500 feet elevation are rare in canyon country. This makes most canyons and many of the mesalands accessible to the experienced hiker who is not discouraged by light snow. In fact, the unusual beauty of snow in redrock country makes winter hiking an aesthetic delight, particularly along the major river gorges.

Plant and Animal Communities

INTRODUCTION

Canyon country is divided by elevation into five general plant communities, four of them somewhat overlapping. The plant communities to some extent control wild animal distribution, although a few adaptable species are found in several or all communities. In addition to the five general plant-animal communities based upon elevation, there are several special life communities, plus seasonal plant variations and animal migrations, all of which add to the experience of hiking in canyon country. It is interesting to note that researchers have concluded that plant and animal sub-species in the La Sal and Abajo mountains are more closely related to similar species in the Rocky Mountains to the east, than to those in the ranges to the west and north within Utah. In fact, certain sub-species found in the La Sals and Abajos are not found west of the Colorado-Green river gorge at all. These distribution anomalies clearly show what an effective barrier that gorge is to land animal distribution. Similarly, the Colorado River gorge within southeastern Utah served as a natural barrier between two prehistoric Indian tribes, the Fremont and the Anasazi, although there was some minor trade and cultural exchange between the tribes across the gorge.

GENERAL COMMUNITIES

Pinyon-Juniper, 3500 to 7500 feet. The principal plant life in this community is pinyon pine, Utah juniper, sagebrush species, blackbrush, greasewood, mountain mahogany, rabbitbrush, Mormon tea, desert holly, cliffrose, saltbush, snakeweed, pad and barrel cactus, yucca and a variety of grasses, small plants and animals. Animal life is quite diverse and includes several species of mice, rats, chipmunks, squirrels and rabbits as well as the coyote, porcupine, mule deer, desert bighorn sheep, ringtailed cat, fox, puma, badger, black bear, ferret, weasel, skunk, prairie dog, marten, pocket gopher, bobcat, pronghorn antelope and a variety of lizards, snakes and amphibians. Some of these, such as ferrets, pumas and bears are rare. Still other plant and animal species live in special communities within this elevation range. These are listed later.

Gambel's oak, 7000 to 8500 feet. The principal plant life in this community is Gambel's oak, mountain mahogany, aspen, squaw bush, several other brushy species, a few species of cacti, snowberry, serviceberry, gooseberry, wild strawberry, raspberry, at least one species of tiny succulent, and a large variety of grasses, low plants and annuals. Red-barked manzanita bush is also found in a few places. It seems to be slowly invading from high country to the east. Animal life consists of species of shrew, mice, chipmunks, rabbits, gophers, moles, badgers and squirrels, as well as other species with wide ranges, such as the porcupine, coyote, mule deer, bear, weasel, bobcat, skunk and ferret. Special communities within this altitude range will be listed later.

Populus, 8000 to 10,500 feet. The principal plant life in this community consists of quaking aspen, willow, conifers such as spruce, fir and a few Ponderosa pines, plus sedge and a wide variety of other shrubs, grasses and annuals. Animal life includes mice, marmots, chipmunks, shrews, voles, muskrats, weasels, mink, wolverines and elk, plus such wide-range species as the porcupine, beaver, coyote, deer, bear, bobcat and skunk. Some of these species are quite rare, but still seen occasionally. Special communities within this altitude range will be listed later.

Conifer, 10,000 to 12,000 feet. The principal plant life in this community is spruce and fir, with some carryover of other species from lower elevations. The animals in this altitude range are also similar to the lower elevations, such as bear, elk, deer, certain small rodents, marmot, porcupine and some of the smaller predators. Special communities within this altitude range will be listed later.

Alpine tundra, 12,000 feet and higher. The principal types of plants in this community are grasses, sedges and the low-growing plants typical of alpine tundra, plus a limited variety of animals. Animal life is far more limited than at lower elevations, but includes pika, marmot, mouse, vole and chipmunk in addition to a few bird species.

SPECIAL COMMUNITIES

Desert grasslands. Within the general pinyon-juniper community of 3500 to 7500 feet elevation, there are areas dominated by desert grasses and low shrubs, with few trees or larger plants. Such seemingly barren areas still support a surprising amount of animal life, principally reptiles, rodents, birds and small predators.

Blackbrush. This special community also lies within the general pinyon-juniper community but is characterized by broad, sandy areas dominated by low-growing blackbrush plus a few grasses, low shrubs, scattered trees and annuals. Here, too, animal life is present, proving the extreme adaptability of desert dwellers.

Aerial. Canyon country is rich in bird life and offers bird watchers plenty of thrills. Various types of birds frequent their typical habitat, with a few species ranging widely throughout the various elevations and special communities. Species commonly seen around water are ducks, geese, egrets, grebes, redwing blackbirds, ouzels, bitterns, killdeer, snipes, sandpipers, curlews, gulls, kingfishers, and herons. Some of these nest in the riverbank marshlands. Raptors include golden and bald eagles, hawks, falcons, owls and several lesser species.

18

Other birds seen are robins, sparrows, starlings, warblers, woodpeckers, bluebirds, jays, nuthatches, grouse, partridges, pheasants, finches, turkey vultures, larks, swifts, wrens, swallows, grosbeaks, hummingbirds, flycatchers, crows, chickadees, titmice, mockingbirds, catbirds, thrashers, thrushes, waxwings, shrikes, vireos, blackbirds, cowbirds, tanagers, doves, ravens, juncoes, orioles, quail, magpies and many others less well known. Several species of bats are also common. The presence of such a variety of birds and bats testifies to the amount of insect life that thrives in high desert regions. Some of the larger insects common to various ecosystems within canyon country are moths, butterflies, beetles and dragonflies.

Riverbank. The banks of the four major rivers in canyon country are special life communities dominated by riverwillows, tamarisk (saltbush), grasses and a variety of water-loving shrubs and animals. Water birds and beaver are common, in addition to small rodents, deer, a few snake species, frogs, toads, salamanders and a variety of small predators. In some locations, stands of scrub oak have grown to unusual size.

Rivers. Canyon country rivers contain several species each of catfish, carp, chub, suckers and shiners, as well as single species of bluegill, sunfish, perch and bass. Some of these are not native to the region's rivers. Certain species of chub, sucker and squawfish are found only in the upper Colorado and lower Green rivers. Of these, the Colorado squawfish, bonytail and humpback chub and humpback sucker are considered rare and endangered species. Water birds such as grebes, ducks and herons are also seen on the rivers, and beaver are fairly common.

Canyon streams. These unique waterways often support unusual communities of life, depending upon whether their flow is perennial or intermittent. Perennial streams generally support willow, tamarisk, watercress, poison oak, nettles, cottonwoods, cattails and other water-loving vegetation, and are frequented by beaver, small fish species, amphibians, birds and garter snake species. Intermittent or seasonal streams support a smaller variety of plant and animal life. Regular visitors to canyon streams include almost every animal species that ranges in the surrounding communities, with the exception of the few rodents adapted to life entirely without ground water.

Lakes and reservoirs. Most canyon country lakes are small, man-made reservoirs, some constructed by pioneer ranchers so long ago that they are not noted in official records, but there are a few small natural lakes in the La Sals and Abajos. Most reservoirs and lakes in the higher elevations contain trout and other fish species. Most are surrounded by water-loving vegetation and are frequented by birds, amphibians, garter snakes, muskrats and an occasional beaver. They are also visited by other animals seeking water to drink. Reservoirs, or stock-ponds as they are often called, built in lower elevations generally play host to tamarisk shrubs, amphibians and a variety of thirsty birds and animals from the surrounding desert. Upper Lake Powell, which is within the region covered by this book, also contains a large variety of lake and river fish species, including minnow species, trout, catfish, sunfish, carp, bluegill, suckers, crappie, bass, shad, northern pike and others. Waterbirds are on and around the lake, and free-swimming beaver that have adapted to lake life are also common in the upper ends of side canyons that are fed by streams.

Marsh. There are several large areas of marshland adjacent to the Colorado, Green and San Juan rivers in canyon country. These wetlands host beaver, waterbirds, amphibians, small fish species, snakes, insects, cottonwoods, tamarisk, willow, cattails and a wide variety of other water-loving plants, and help support several species of predatory birds and animals.

Spring-seep caves. These unique caves or alcoves in sandstone are fairly common in canyon country, although rare elsewhere. The wet or dripping rock walls, often with pools of crystal-clear water below them, create small, isolated ecosystems of water-loving life. Lichens, mosses, ferns, orchids, columbines and other such plants cling to the walls and grow on the rocks below the drips or around the pools. Poison oak often thrives below such caves, as do other moisture-loving plants and animals. Certain types of moss-like vegetation sometimes hang in festoons from the moist rock walls. The water in such seeps is generally biologically pure, although it may contain minerals. A few caves contain pools large and deep enough to offer hikers a cooling dip.

Potholes. The myriad slickrock potholes in canyon country sometimes contain tiny ecosystems all their own, life that is entirely unique to desert sandstone country. Such potholes are formed by infrequent wetting-drying cycles, with wind removing the water-loosened sand from the bottom of the holes during dry periods. Some reach such a size that they accumulate unremoved sand, which holds the rare moisture and eventually supports conventional desert plants and animals. Other potholes, with only thin sediments in their bottoms, on rare occasions receive enough water to support the odd life cycles of desert shrimp, fairy shrimp, clam shrimp, young amphibians, algae and other specially adapted microlife. When enough water accumulates in such rare potholes, and lasts long enough during warm weather, long-dormant generations of microlife hatch from the wet sediments and go through frantic life cycles of eating each other, breeding, and laying new eggs in the mud, all within a few days. The most fascinating of these novel creatures is the desert shrimp, which resembles a tiny, soft horseshoe crab and may grow to an overall length of three inches. They are propelled through the water by a multitude of cilia on their undersides, and at first glance resemble gray-green tadpoles. During dry spells, which may last for years, the eggs of pothole life-forms suffer high attrition from dehydration beyond their tolerance, and from small rodents that dig up and eat the larger eggs. The hiker who is lucky enough to find one of these special potholes during its wet-life cycle can plan on spending quite a bit of time in the prone position, closely watching the fascinating activity in its tiny lake of desert-warm water.

Cryptogamic soil. Much of the soil in canyon country below the 8000-foot level is very sandy because of the predominance of decomposing sandstone. Oddly, however, except in actual wash bottoms or where it has been disturbed by the activities of humans or domestic animals, this sandy soil is moved very little by rain and wind erosion. Living (shifting) sand dunes are relatively rare in even the sandiest areas of canyon country. The reason for this is what scientists call "cryptogamic soil." In simple terms, this means that certain very hardy, slow-growing species of microscopic plant life grow and thrive within the top two or three inches of sand or sandy soil. The fine, threadlike rootlets and fibers of these microflora literally bind together the loose sand. In appearance, cryptogamic soil looks like a dark, corrugated or lumpy crust on top of sand or sandy soil. This crust is fragile, easily broken and destroyed by tires, bulldozer tracks and blades, human feet, and the hooves of domestic livestock. Once such crusts are broken, they take years to mend, and during that time wind and water erosion is drastically accelerated. In essence, cryptogamic soil is the very basis of the dominant ecosystems within canyon country. Hikers who do not wish to disturb the delicate balance of these desert ecosystems will avoid damaging areas of cryptogamic soil whenever possible.

SEASONAL CHANGES

Plant life. Canyon country seasonal variations bring corresponding changes in plant life. The majority of the perennial plants and trees go dormant in the winter, although many species adapted to arid life do not lose their foliage. Pinyon, juniper, sage and blackbrush change little in appearance year around, as do the mountain conifers. In the early spring, other species burgeon into fresh life. New leaves add bright greens to deciduous trees and shrubs, while grasses and hundreds of species of annual wildflowers contribute vivid hues to canyons and desert areas. As the season progresses to higher elevations, still other species leaf out and add floral beauty to their surroundings. Most wildflower displays below 6000 feet are gone by late spring, but some species, such as sunflowers, are then just starting. Late summer usually brings thundershowers, and this moisture triggers the blooming cycles of still other annuals and shrubs. Rabbitbrush and snakeweed add vivid patches of yellow to all the lower elevations. There is probably more sheer mass of wildflower color during the canyon country autumn than in the spring, except when the previous winter has been exceptionally wet. Early autumn also turns aspen golden, scrub oak into various shades of red, yellow, amber and brown, and other mountain plants into other bright shades of color. Fall colors in the La Sals and Abajos are almost always brilliant. Late autumn sees the cottonwoods in the lower elevations turn golden, and the feathery tamarisk beside water courses or pools also assumes shades of yellow and amber. Despite all this seasonal dormancy, however, much of canyon country changes very little in appearance year around. Pinyon-juniper forests and areas dominated by blackbrush seem the same in any season, unless they bear a light coat of snow. All of which adds up to delightful year-around hiking.

Animal life. Some canyon country deer and elk migrate to lower elevations in the winter. Most deer, however, live year around below the worst snow levels. Birds, of course, follow their customary migration patterns, but some species stay in canyon country all year. Only the worst winters give these any problems. All reptiles, amphibians and many of the smaller mammals hibernate, which leaves predators less than well fed. Even so, it is common in the winter to see the tracks of small animals and predators in the snow. Observant hikers can sometimes read violent stories where such tracks converge. Since, of all the wildlife in canyon country, only certain birds leave the region in the winter, severe winters exact a heavy toll of all animals that do not hibernate, and even some of these may freeze. Nonetheless, enough of all species survive each winter to renew their complex cycles of life the following spring, cycles that are admirably adapted to the seasonal extremes of canyon country.

Services, Facilities, Supplies and Access

In canyon country, sources of visitor services, facilities and supplies are few and widely separated. With few exceptions, the sources that exist are in the communities located on or near U.S. 163, the main highway through canyon country. The larger communities of Moab, Monticello and Blanding provide most traveler amenities. The smaller settlements of Crescent Junction, La Sal Junction, La Sal, Fry Canyon, Bluff, Mexican Hat and Hite offer only very limited services, facilities and supplies.

There is no scheduled air service into the region covered by this book, but there are public air fields near Moab, Monticello, Blanding, Bluff, Mexican Hat and Hite. Most of these air fields offer either car rentals or some kind of transport to the nearest town.

Access to canyon country by train or bus is very limited. AMTRAC trains stop at Thompson, six miles east of Crescent Junction on the business loop of I-70. Commercial buses travel U.S. 163 through part of canyon country, but do not go to all communities. Check bus company offices for current schedules, routes and towns served.

While hitchhiking is not encouraged in southeastern Utah, it is not illegal if certain limitations are observed. It is not legal to wait for rides on Interstate freeways such as I-70, nor on the pavement or shoulders of U.S. or State highways. The Utah State Highway Patrol advises hitchhikers to wait for rides on freeway approaches, where it is safe for motorists to stop, and well off of the pavement and shoulders of other highways. For the most part, hitchhiking is safe and fairly easy on most rural Utah highways, and is a mode of travel widely used by young adults carrying backpacks during the warmer seasons. During the late fall, winter and early spring, vehicle traffic on canyon country highways is generally too light, and the weather too cool, for practical hitchhiking.

Types of Hiking

Because of the unique and relatively undeveloped nature of canyon country, there are several distinct types of hiking there, most of them to be found nowhere else in the country. With each trail listed in this book, the trail type is noted. The designated hiking trails listed are comprehensive for the region covered at the time of publication, but the other hiking routes listed are merely representative of the non-designated types of hiking available. There are many other routes for each type, but the ones listed will serve to introduce hikers to the variety of hiking that canyon country offers.

Designated trails. All three land administration agencies within canyon country provide some form of designated hiking trails, although one, the U.S. Forest Service, devotes little budget or effort to the maintenance and marking of established trails. The National Park Service provides by far the majority of all designated hiking trails in canyon country. All are within the region's parks or monuments, and all are well maintained and marked.

Mountain hiking. Mountain hiking in canyon country is much the same as in other mountains, except that the La Sals and Abajos have very few designated trails, and these are poorly maintained and marked, making them difficult to follow. Hiking should not be limited to such trails, however. Both ranges are laced with off-road vehicle trails. Some of these are maintained and traveled with fair frequency, but most are poorly maintained, if at all, and traveled rarely. Some have become so overgrown by dense vegetation, or blocked by landslides or fallen trees, that they are no longer usable by vehicles. For practical purposes, hikers can use such abandoned or infrequently traveled vehicle trails as hiking trails. They sometimes go through terrain where the vegetation is too dense for cross-country hiking. For hikers who disdain all vehicle trails, the intermediate elevations in canyon country mountains will prove a challenge because of dense brush, very steep slopes and deeply cut gorges. The highest elevations provide somewhat easier going, but slopes of loose rubble offer another kind of problem.

Canyon rim hiking. This type of canyon country hiking is spectacular and challenging. Rim hiking routes follow canyon rims continuously, deviating only when forced to by impassable terrain. Rim hiking requires that the hiker go up the rim of each branching sidecanyon, then back again to the main canyon. Thus, hiking the rim of a complex canyon system can take days, and place heavy demands upon the hiker, but the challenge of staying with a rim, and the continuous breathtaking spectacle of the canyons unfolding below, are ample rewards for persistence. Canyon rim hiking is one of the highlights of canyon country hiking.

24

Slickrock hiking. Slickrock hiking is unique to the Four Corners region. Nowhere else are there such extensive and weirdly-eroded masses of stone. Slickrock hiking offers unique rewards and challenges, and places a premium upon free-climbing skills. There are many places in canyon country where huge areas of almost barren sandstone are eroded into low domes and complex mazes of shallow arroyos and canyons. In other areas, closely packed giant fins or long, twisting ridges of almost totally bare sandstone loom high above the surrounding terrain. Only on foot can such slickrock regions be explored, and trying to follow a slickrock ridge or cross an area of massive fins and domes can offer a challenge to any hiker. Those who seriously accept that challenge will sometimes find free-climbing skills, and even rapelling equipment and experience, useful.

Canyon-stream hiking. Exploring a deep and complex canyon system by the simple expedience of following its wash bottoms can be very rewarding, but especially so if the main canyon contains a continuous or intermittent stream. There are many such in canyon country, despite its semi-arid nature, especially in the lower "foothills" of the La Sal and Abajo ranges. A few such canyons are worth hiking for 20 to 40 miles. Some well-watered canyons offer hikers glimpses of prehistoric civilizations in addition to the usual natural history highlights. Canyon-stream hiking is especially pleasant during the warmer months, because the springs, pools and streams provide practical cooling as well as aesthetic enjoyment and more profuse plant and animal life. Some stream-watered canyons contain unique lifeforms and ecosystems, such as a species of scentless, night-blooming primrose that grows six to eight feet tall, or spring-formed grottoes with communities of fern, orchids and other water-loving life. A few canyon streams even support species of tiny fish. Hiking desert canyons can be a challenge because of sheer or terraced drops which are often difficult to bypass. Hikers who intend to follow certain canyons for their entire lengths will find free-climbing and rapelling skills and equipment necessary, yet those who pursue such challenges will be amply rewarded for their efforts. Hiking the sandstone desert canyons of this region is a unique experience.

Lakeside hiking. Lakes in canyon country are not common but do exist. There are a number of small natural lakes and man-made reservoirs in the La Sal and Abajo mountains. These all offer short-range but interesting shoreline hiking. There is a somewhat larger lake on the eastern slopes of the La Sals, just east of the Colorado-Utah border. Some of these small mountain lakes, such as Oowah in the La Sals, have foot trails around them established by generations of sportsmen, but not designated or maintained by the Forest Service. For the most part, lakeside hiking in canyon country mountains is primitive hiking. The lower elevations offer a novel type of lakeshore hiking at Lake Powell. Boats, and a few roads, offer access to the shores of this unique desert lake. Hikers who overlook this novel experience will miss one highlight of canyon country hiking. Because of the nature of lakeside hiking in this region, it is not practical or necessary to list individual hiking routes in the trails section of this book.

Riverbank hiking. It is not possible to hike the entire length of the four river gorges in canyon country; the Green, Colorado, San Juan and Dolores. Sheer walls at the rivers' edges, dense vegetation and great rockfalls make passage even on foot either impossible or so difficult and dangerous that it is not worth the effort. Even so, it is possible to hike many long stretches of these rivers. In some places, abandoned or rarely used off-road vehicle trails can serve as hiking trails. In other stretches, long-established deer trails show hikers the easiest route through rough or overgrown terrain. Access to good riverbank hiking stretches can be a problem. Highways, roads and off-road vehicle trails provide easy access to some, but others are accessible only by boat or raft of some sort. Swimming the Green, San Juan or Colorado in order to bypass hiking hazards or to cross to the other side can be extremely dangerous and is not recommended, even during low-water periods. Except during the high-water months, or following heavy rains, it is generally safe to wade the Dolores in many places. In canyon country, riverbank hiking offers access to areas that can be explored no other way, including dozens of completely natural and unspoiled side canyons. Due to the nature of riverbank hiking in canyon country, it is not practical to list hikable stretches of the rivers or access routes in the trails section of this book.

Winter hiking. Except during occasional brief storms, canyon country winters offer endless hiking opportunities. In the lower elevations, daytime temperatures are often well above freezing, with little or no snow. Higher elevations will have more snow and be colder. In most winters, hiking is possible almost anywhere below 6500 feet. Much of the region covered by this book is below that elevation. Above 6500, snowshoe hiking and cross-country skiing are still practical. Because of the heavily wooded, steep nature of canyon country mountain ranges, the best winter hiking and skiing routes are the vehicle roads and trails. Although these are closed and impassable to wheeled vehicles in the winter, most remain passable to snowshoe hikers or cross-country skiers with the desire, equipment, skills, and stamina.

Hiking Hazards

Hiking in canyon country is unlike hiking anywhere else. The unique nature of the terrain, its climate and wildlife, present unique problems and exaggerate others normal to more conventional hiking. Even hikers highly experienced in many kinds of terrain will find it useful to study the following problems and suggested special precautions before setting out to explore the wild beauty of canyon country.

The land. In comparison with most of this nation, canyon country is very rugged, remote and undeveloped. Human settlements are few and widely scattered, and except for the few main highways, the roads are infrequently traveled. On many backcountry roads, vehicles may not be seen for days or even weeks. This may be excellent for undisturbed wilderness hiking, but presents a serious problem when hikers get lost or injured, or run low on vital supplies. It is thus important to hiking safety that before setting out to hike anywhere in canyon country, except on the few well-traveled, designated trails, hikers tell someone where they are going, their approximate route and anticipated time or day of return. This should be followed up by checking back with the notified person or agency upon return. Otherwise, that person or agency should automatically alert the appropriate search and rescue organization. Except in national parks, this is generally done by notifying the county sheriff. In national parks, any park ranger or employee will initiate search and rescue action. Hikers in need of help should follow standard procedures of waiting in a place clearly visible to air searchers, and making that place more noticeable by means of a smoky fire or other signalling device. It is also advisable to hike in groups of two or more, so that in case of accident at least one person will be able to administer first aid and then seek help. Every hiker should carry a well-supplied first aid kit.

Water. Hikers accustomed to mountain hiking and plentiful pure water for drinking must beware of canyon country hiking, especially during the warmer months. Canyon country mountains present few problems with potable water, but the lower country is another matter. There are occasionally springs and streams in canyon bottoms, but water elsewhere is very rare. Further, with the exception of flowing springs at their sources, the water that is found should not be considered potable without boiling or chemical treatment. Grazing domestic livestock in many areas contaminate surface water beyond safe human use, and the flow is insufficient for natural purification by aeration. In some areas, springs and streams are so highly mineralized that they can cause severe gastro-intestinal problems or even poisoning. Signs of such bad water are taste and mineral buildup at the water's edge. It is thus important that hikers carry along all of their drinking water, unless they know in advance that there will be sufficient potable water along their anticipated route. This is vitally important in non-mountainous canyon country regions, especially during the warmer months. As a general rule of thumb, each hiker should carry at least one gallon of water for each day of hiking during warm weather, perhaps less when it is cooler. Buffered salt tablets are also recommended during the summer. Hikers should be aware that due to the normal low humidity of canyon country in all seasons, considerable body fluid can be lost without the hiker's awareness of the loss. Perspiration may dry without being noticed, thus negating one of the normal warnings of excessive water loss. It is thus critical that canyon country hikers always carry and drink enough water. The scarcity of potable water in canyon country and the resultant necessity for carrying all the water needed, places a severe limit on the length of backpacking trips, except in the mountains and along canyon systems that contain reliable sources of water. The lack of readily available water along arid hiking routes also reduces the value of carrying dehydrated meals on overnight hikes, because the water must be carried for rehydration of such foods before their use.

Navigation. Canyon country is a land of extremes when it comes to surface geography. Canyons, gorges, hazardous rivers, unscaleable rock walls and impenetrable masses of slickrock present obstacles to straightforward hiking and navigation. Unprepared hikers may find themselves barred from further progress by these natural hazards, and have to backtrack for many miles. It is thus recommended that

hikers who plan to sample more than the few designated trails in canyon country acquire, learn to read, and carry with them topographic maps of the area to be explored. A compass is also helpful but not essential. The most useful and easily available topographic maps are the 1:62,500 series, or about one mile to the inch, issued by the U.S. Geological Survey. These are available through any U.S.G.S. office directly or by mail. Topo maps of the region covered by this book can usually be obtained at the federal land administration offices in Moab and Monticello. Special topographic maps of Arches and Canyonlands National Parks and vicinity, drawn to similar scale, may be purchased at any Park Service visitor center or office in canyon country, The U.S. Forest Service issues maps of the canyon country national forests. Although these show the approximate locations of major features, vehicle trails and hiking routes, their usefulness is quite limited because they do not show surface contours.

Temperature extremes and sun. As noted earlier, the high desert and mountains of canyon country sometimes reach temperature extremes at both ends of the scale. Such extremes can be hazardous to hikers who are not prepared. During very cold weather, it is important to wear enough of the right type of clothing. This subject has been adequately covered in books on skiing and other winter sports. Choice of proper clothing is also important for hot weather hiking, especially in sunny, arid desert country. Unless the hiker is darkly tanned, light-weight, light-colored clothing should cover body, arms and legs, and a wide-brimmed, well ventilated hat should be worn to protect the head and neck. Even tanned hikers should carry and use a good protective sun lotion. In canyon country, the sun is bright at all elevations, and in most of the region reflective rock and sand add to the sun's intensity. It is better to wear protective clothing and lotions than to have a wonderful hike spoiled by painful sunburn.

Venomous reptiles. There are several species of snakes and many species of lizards in canyon country, but venomous snakes are rare. There are no poisonous lizards. In the canyon-mesa areas, one rare species of rattlesnake called the "midget faded rattler" is occasionally seen, but is so small and shy it seldom poses a danger to humans. It is generally less than two feet long. In the more open meadows and sage flats, larger species of rattlers help keep rodents in balance. Rattlers are rare in the mountains. To avoid danger from rattlesnakes, hikers should wear high-top leather boots and avoid placing hands or feet near where snakes might be hiding; that is, in dense brush or under rocks or ledges. A snake-bite kit and knowledge of snake-bite first aid is also recommended for those planning backcountry hikes. Hikers who do encounter snakes, including rattlers, should bear in mind that these hardy reptiles all have a place in nature. "Live and let live" is a good motto for hikers to apply to all wildlife. For those especially interested in snakes, one species fairly common to canyon country is the bullsnake, a close relative if not identical to the California gopher snake. These beautiful, rodent-eating reptiles are quite easy to capture and, with gentle handling, become quite tame. They do not thrive in captivity, however, so should be released after a few minutes of study.

Other wildlife. As noted earlier, wildlife abounds in canyon country but, as in many desert regions, much of it is nocturnal and rarely seen. The only wild animals in canyon country that may be hazardous to hikers, other than rattlesnakes, are skunks and porcupines. These creatures are well protected by nature and, if surprised at close range, can spoil an otherwise pleasant hike. Bears have been seen in the mountain ranges, but are too rare to be a problem. Mountain-ranging deer and elk could be a hazard during their breeding seasons, but again the probability of such an encounter is very low. In canyon country as in all wilderness regions, however, hikers should always be alert for non-typical behavior among wild animals, because this often means danger from individuals infected by diseases such as rabies. This is extremely rare but does occur.

Dangerous plantlife. Canyon country has the same hazardous desert plants that occur in most other southwestern desert regions, such as barrel and pad cacti and sharp-tipped yucca leaves. In addition, there are patches of nettles in well watered mountain areas, and some of the wetter streams and spring-seep caves in the canyons have growths of poison oak. To avoid annoying and painful contact with these plants, hikers should be able to identify them, be on the alert and avoid all contact. Even clothing or boots contaminated by nettles or poison oak, or full of cactus spines, can later transfer these irritants to human skin. Canyon country also has many edible species of fruit, berries and seeds, but there are also some quite poisonous. Again, proper identification is important before any wild plant product is eaten. The best rule is — if in doubt, don't eat it.

Dangerous and annoying insects. There are three species of venomous insects in canyon country; scorpions, tarantulas and black widow spiders. The scorpions and tarantulas are rare and are only mildly venomous species. Hikers may spend months in the back country without seeing a single specimen of either. Black widows are more common but, due to their shy nature, are rarely seen. Their characteristic haphazard webs are often found under dry rock ledges or in shallow caves, but the spider is almost always out of sight hidden in a narrow crack. During the warmer seasons, and in certain places, mosquitos, gnats and small biting flies can be annoying to hikers. Riverbanks, stream-watered canyons and the mountains in the summer are the worst for mosquitoes, but gnats and flies can be almost anywhere. A few areas have a species of biting gnat. A good "deep-woods" insect repellant cream will discourage gnats, flies and mosquitoes, and should be carried in every hiker's pack.

Domestic livestock. Even the most remote areas of canyon country are generally under lease for the grazing of domestic livestock. Cattle are the most common, but herds of sheep may be encountered. With the possible exception of an occasional irritable old bull, or an overly protective cow with a calf, such animals pose little danger to hikers. Hikers can, however, be dangerous to livestock by frightening them so that they injure themselves on the rough terrain. Because of this, hikers should always avoid approaching or startling any domestic animals they may encounter.

Hazardous terrain. Canyon country terrain is big, rough and full of natural hazards. Except on established trails, hiking is almost always far more than just straightforward walking. It generally involves considerable climbing and scrambling over rocks, through gullies and among trees, and may also require a certain amount of free-climbing, using both hands and feet. Some of the more challenging routes will also require light climbing gear and skills. Most hiking routes require considerable up and down travel. All of these natural hazards mean that canyon country hiking demands far more strength and endurance than more conventional hiking. Those not in top physical condition should limit their hikes accordingly, so as to avoid serious problems with over-exertion and exhaustion. Two special hazards deserve careful attention. The sheer or steep cliffs common to canyon country lower elevations are very dangerous. Hikers who attempt to scale even low cliffs can easily get "rim-rocked," that is, unable to go up or down. Extreme caution, climbing equipment, and experience are essential if cliff-scaling is to be attempted. The mountains present another hazard. Large slopes of loose rock can start sliding with avalanche force if hikers attempt to cross them. Such slopes should be avoided.

Flash-flooding. All desert areas are prone to flash-flooding. Wherever watersheds are relatively bare of vegetation and water-holding soil, rain from heavy generalized storms or localized thunderhead clouds is not held and runs off, accumulating very rapidly to torrential levels. In canyon country this process is still further exaggerated by steep mountain flanks, drastically tilted geologic strata and ground surfaces that may to a large extent be solid sandstone. Highly destructive and dangerous flash floods are hence to be expected whenever any appreciable amount of rain falls upon an area too fast for its ability to absorb the water. Further, since much of the rain that falls in canyon country comes from great thunderhead cloud systems that drift across the land leaving a relatively narrow band of precipitation, it is quite common for a flash flood to go roaring down a perfectly dry major canyon miles from any rain, with the water coming from localized precipitation that fell onto the canyon's upper tributary system.

The foothill canyons that drain the Abajo and La Sal mountains are especially prone to flash-flooding because the mountains tend to generate enormous thunderhead systems, which in turn dump heavy precipitation on the mountain flanks and lower highlands, especially to the lee of the mountains. In canyon country, generalized rainstorms are most apt to occur in the spring of the year, while localized thunderhead systems are generated throughout the spring, summer and fall.

Hikers should be continually aware of flash-flood hazards, especially when exploring canyon systems. If clouds indicate there might be rain in the area drained by the canyon, hikers should stay out of stretches that are between close, sheer canyon walls and should hike on higher ground above the wash bottom. Further, no matter how placid the weather may seem, hikers should never camp overnight in or even near a canyon stream or drywash, no matter how delightful the setting may be. Those who might doubt the value of this advice should make it a point to study the wash along the lower end of any long canyon system, such as Cane Creek Canyon, and take note of the water-borne driftwood and debris left by the last big flood, perched on big boulders and rocky shelves six, eight or even ten feet above the innocent-seeming and bone-dry wash bottom. Anyone who has actually witnessed the sheer mindless ferocity of a canyon country flash flood, and who has seen how quickly it can appear and grow, will never again need to be reminded to beware of desert-canyon flash-flooding.

Discovery Highlights

To those who have never visited southeastern Utah's canyon country, the entire region will be a place of wondrous new things, of scenes never before imagined. A few of the region's major highlights are widely recognized and protected within national or state parks, monuments, historic sites and primitive or recreation areas, but countless other areas or sites are little known and receive no special protection.

In addition to its large and easily discovered wonders, canyon country offers innumerable delightful smaller rewards to those with the interest and persistence to seek them out. The country is so large and broken by surface erosion and geologic effects that it is still possible for backcountry hikers to make original discoveries, some even of scientific importance. Some places and things may have historic or prehistoric significance. Others may have value only for their unique beauty, or as examples of unusual ecosystems, natural processes or wildlife adaptability. Following are just a few of the types of special highlights for which backcountry hikers should be alert.

Wildlife is rarely seen, except for deer, birds and diurnal rodents, but foot tracks in sand or mud can often tell curious stories, or tell of unseen animals. Finding cacti or wildflowers in bloom, edible fruit, berries or nuts, or such exotic blooming plants as datura or night-blooming primrose is always rewarding. Spring-seep caves, especially those with dripping water, always offer insights into unusual, isolated ecosystems.

Remnants of the human past are always interesting. Prehistoric rock and log structures, petroglyph and pictograph panels, chipping grounds and hunting camps are scattered throughout canyon country. Old pioneer structures such as log or rock cabins, wagon bridges and roads, small reservoirs, long abandoned corrals, cowboy camps, old mines and ghost mining communities can also be found in many places, some of them with no recorded history.

Strange erosional forms are myriad, and even today there are occasional reports of newly discovered natural arches, bridges and windows. Other natural features such as caves, large slickrock potholes, balanced rocks, water-carved grottoes, spires, and narrow but passable rock crevices are always fun to find, as are exceptionally large, lovely or deep canyon pools or streams. Breathtakingly spectacular canyon rim overlooks are common, yet each one encountered has something special to offer. Quite often, slickrock canyon rims, especially the higher ones, are ablaze with patches of colorful lichens.

Prehistoric remnants of life are always fascinating. Many of the geologic strata common to canyon country are rich lodes of sealife fossils, petrified wood, fossilized bone and curious mineral specimens. The richest formations are, starting with the oldest, the Rico (marine fossils), Chinle (marine fossils, petrified wood, minerals), Morrison (marine fossils, petrified wood and bone, minerals) and Dakota (fossil

Stiles

plants and wood, minerals), but most other strata contain at least a few things of interest. Kayenta Sandstone may contain dinosaur tracks as may several younger strata. Moenkopi and Kayenta both contain beautiful ripplerock and mud casts.

It can thus be seen that hiking in canyon country is not just simple walking from one point to another. It is tougher and more demanding, but also infinitely more rewarding than conventional hiking elsewhere.

Hiking Areas

The region covered by this book is broken into several distinct areas by formidable natural barriers and by major roads and highways. The western boundary of this region, the Colorado-Green river gorge, was chosen because of accessibility factors. Access to the areas west of this gorge is from roads still farther west. There is no access to the west side of the gorge from its east side between the settlements of Green River and Hite, Utah, on upper Lake Powell. Conversely, the region covered by this book is accessible only from highways, roads and vehicle trails on the east side of the Colorado-Green gorge.

Similarly, practical access routes, as well as natural geographic barriers, have determined the outlines of the hiking areas formalized in this book. Maps with each section of the book show these areas and the principal approaches to them. The introduction to each area discusses practical locations for base camps from which to explore that area. Directions with each trail tell how to find the trailheads from the road approaches. For convenience, each hiking area has been given a name based upon some major geologic feature within that area.

Broom

The sandy canyon floor was fascinating, an open-air museum of animal tracks, often quite distinct where the sand was moist near springs, or below where desert water courses dropped over the high rim into the canyon.

Lower Sevenmile Canyon showed all the signs of abundant wildlife. Water, at intervals in Sevenmile and in Courthouse Wash on down, was one attraction. The lack of human intrusion was another. We had seen no other traces of humanity since dropping into the deep canyon at its boxed upper end near the highway, except for an occasional piece of milled but very weathered wood, obviously washed down from the higher, developed reaches of Sevenmile by some long-ago flash flood.

The tiny tracks in the sandy wash told tales, some of them violent. The slithery trail of a lizard would intersect the multiple tracks of a plodding beetle—but only the reptile's tracks would continue, leaving a little scuffled area where the two trails converged.

Some tracks would start and end magically—birds.

We ambled down the canyon, past great sun-bleached driftwood logs and patches of living sand dunes, admiring the unspoiled canyon beauty and reading the signs of life all around us.

There were the tracks of a fox, a pocket squirrel, a cottontail, a snake. These were made by a raven, those by a doe and fawn. Here, a badger had dug for some luckless rodent, there a coyote had sniffed around another small burrow. And this was where a broom had walked along the wash bottom—

A broom!?

We looked more closely at the odd pattern in the fine, dry sand—curving, overlapping whisk-broom marks, punctuated by featureless dents in the sand that had been obscured by the "broom".

Puzzled, we hurried along the unfamiliar trail, looking for further clues. Several hundred yards on down the wash, it entered a brushy stretch and became difficult to follow. But we persisted, our curiosity overcoming our aversion to duck-walking under overhanging tamarisk, willow and larger tree limbs.

The trail left the wash and cut through the brush toward a fifty-foot cottonwood, still bare of leaves in this late-winter season.

And there was our "broom", perched high in the tree, wedged into a crotch and looking stolidly down at us out of black, beady eyes. A huge porcupine!

But in a cottonwood? Since porcupines prefer the bark of pinyon to that of a cottonwood, especially one in its dormant stage, this big fellow must have heard us hot on his trail and sought altitude for safety. And there he was, twenty feet above us but clearly visible—our well-defended friend with a broom for a tail.

Canyon Country

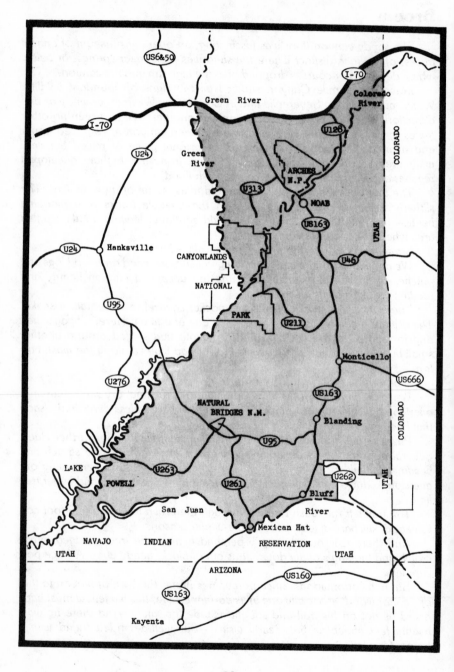

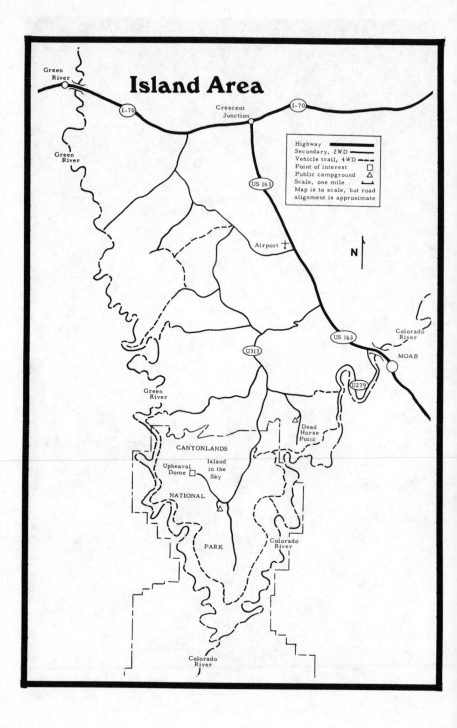

Island Area

Island Area

AREA NAME: This area was named after Island in the Sky, an elevated, sheer-walled peninsula that dominates the southern part of this area.

AREA BOUNDARIES: Interstate 70, U.S. 163, Colorado River, Green River.

U.S.G.S. TOPOGRAPHIC MAPS THAT COVER THE AREA: Green River, Crescent Junction, Thompson, Bowknot Bend, The Knoll, Moab, The Spur, Upheaval Dome, Hatch Point, The Needles; a 46" by 61" map of Canyonlands National Park and vicinity also covers part of this area.

GENERAL TOPOGRAPHY: high, rolling desert between 4000 and 6500 elevation; bordered on three sides by deep gorges; broken by gigantic rock outcroppings and ridges; slashed by canyons and gorges, especially the southern half.

SUGGESTED BASE CAMPS: motels or commercial campgrounds in Moab or Green River; developed public campgrounds at Dead Horse Point State Park, Green River Overlook in Canyonlands National Park; primitive campgrounds as designated along White Rim Trail; primitive camping is permitted almost anywhere within the area except within Canyonlands National Park and Dead Horse Point State Park; contact park rangers for current regulations in these areas.

ACCESS ROUTES: Interstate 70 (U.S. 6 & 50), U.S. 163, Utah 313, Utah 279, county roads and off-road vehicle trails as shown on area map.

AREA NOTES:
1. The non-designated hiking trails, routes and areas listed are just representative samples of the primitive hiking available in this area.
2. The geologic formations exposed in most of the northern half of this area provide excellent rockhounding.
3. Following normal or wet winters, this area has outstanding displays of wildflowers in early spring.
4. Prehistoric Indian use of this area was very limited, but it does have a few archaeological sites. Most of these are within Canyonlands National Park or the canyons north of the park.

Moses

My wife and I were hiking along a remote canyon rim, looking for a way down its steep slickrock walls into a stretch of canyon that contained pools of water surrounded by lush vegetation.

The rimlands were typical sandflats—rolling, rocky, with lots of sand held in place by cryptogamic soil, low desert shrubs, hardy grasses and a scattering of pinyon and juniper trees. Flat slabs of rock marked the rim above steep, curving slopes of solid sandstone.

We both spotted the anomaly on one such slope at once. "What's that?", my wife asked.

An old and very narrow trail angled down the smooth rock, a trail made by driving short steel pegs into the rock, placing logs against the pegs then building a trail by adding small rocks and soil to the logs. We had seen this type of construction elsewhere in canyon country.

I walked back and forth along the rim, tracing the trail to its upper and lower ends. There were very faint traces of wheel tracks to the top of the trail, tracks made so long ago the desert shrubs had completely recovered. The original trail maker had dug or blasted a notch in the overhanging rim, then worked his way down at an angle across curving slopes of slickrock, making a log trail as he went. Where a log section was not practical, he had laboriously cut steps into the rock. Several sets of these crossed a series of rock-and-sand terraces.

Rock steps down the last few yards of the trail ended in a drywash not far from one of the pools we had spotted from the rim. A little arch marked the lower end of the trail.

As we descended the man-made trail, we examined it closely. No signs of recent use. If it had been built to allow cattle to reach the canyon's water, it had not served this purpose for a long, long time. No scratches in the rock from shod hooves, either. The rock steps were very weathered, with the original pick-marks quite faint.

"Hey, look!" My wife pointed to one of the log-trail pegs. It was a short piece of water pipe, with an old-fashioned faucet still attached to its upper end.

"I wonder if it still works," she said, reaching down to twist futilely at the faucet handle. We both laughed, but to this day I'm not sure whether my good wife's laughter was at her own joke, or from embarrassment at her subconscious expectation of perhaps getting water out of a pipe stuck in solid rock, like a modern, female Moses.

Corona-Bowtie

TYPE OF TRAIL: designated.

TRAIL MILEAGE: about 2 miles round trip.

TIME TO HIKE: about 3 hours.

U.S.G.S. MAP: Moab quadrangle.

HAZARDS: trail poorly marked; old trail that continues beyond Corona Arch up onto the high slickrock is now unsafe except for experienced rock climbers with proper equipment.

SEASONS: best during cooler months of spring or fall, but may be hiked any time, even with snow on the ground.

ACCESS: drive downriver from Moab Valley on Utah 279; about 10 miles from U.S. 163, park at Gold Bar loop of Colorado River near indicated trailhead; follow sign and various trail markings to Corona Arch.

TRAIL SUMMARY: This short but spectacular trail goes to two large and entirely different arches that are within a few yards of each other; an unmarked spur trail around a slickrock terrace goes to a third medium sized arch; the trail offers panoramic views of the Colorado River gorge.

TRAIL HIGHLIGHTS

The trail to Corona and Bowtie climbs abruptly from Utah 279 to cross the rail spur that serves the potash mining operation at the end of the highway. Beyond the rails, the foot trail follows an abandoned vehicle trail up onto a bench below the Navajo Sandstone slickrock cliffs that dominate this part of the Colorado River gorge. Rockhounds will find the ancient river gravel deposits here of interest. Beyond this bench, the trail is poorly marked. The route to Corona and Bowtie is toward the deep canyon to the right, or east, and along the base of the slickrock cliff. Following this cliff to the left will lead to another arch called Pinto, or Gold Bar, that can be seen from the highway and other points. The trail to Corona and Bowtie first offers a glimpse of these spectacular natural spans as it follows a rock terrace around a short canyon spur. Bowtie Arch formed when a big cliff-edge pothole broke through into a spring-seep cave below. Subsequent weathering has created a lovely arch. Corona Arch, or Little Rainbow as it is sometimes called, closely resembles famous Rainbow Bridge, but on a much smaller scale. It formed from a slickrock fin by slow wind-and-water weathering. The return hike along the same route offers spectacular views down into the Colorado River gorge.

NOTES: Hikers should not attempt to get to Corona and Bowtie arches by following the railroad tracks up the canyon toward the tunnel. Climbing up out of the railroad canyon can be very hazardous.

POISON SPIDER - GOLD BAR RIM

TYPE OF TRAIL: canyon rim.

TRAIL MILEAGE: optional, 5 to 15 miles or longer.

TIME TO HIKE: optional, one day or longer.

U.S.G.S. MAP: Moab quadrangle.

HAZARDS: no water; hazardous cliffs.

SEASONS: best during cooler months of spring or fall, but may be hiked in the summer, too.

ACCESS: drive downriver from Moab Valley on Utah 279; first access is via ascending ledges about ¾ mile west of river portal; second access is via off-road vehicle trail at petroglyph-dinosaur track roadside exhibit site, 3 miles west of river portal; alternate access is via off-road vehicle trail beginning at gate 7 miles north of Colorado River bridge on U.S. 163.

TRAIL SUMMARY: This non-designated hiking route along canyon rim slickrock affords breathtaking views down into the Colorado River gorge, Moab Valley, the redrock gorge north of Moab Valley and Little Canyon; an optional route extension affords views of the primitve south fork of Sevenmile Canyon.

TRAIL HIGHLIGHTS

The high eastern rim of Poison Spider Mesa overlooks the town of Moab, the swamps and bottomlands of the Colorado River as it crosses Moab Valley and a broad panorama of sandstone country and mountains to the south and east. The rim continues north to become Gold Bar rim. The elevated red-walled valley called Little Canyon slashes deeply into the high rim, forcing hikers to descend into Little Canyon or retrace their route. If the off-road vehicle trail west of the river portal is used to gain access to the slickrock rim, this adds several miles of beautiful river gorge to the hike, as well as Little Arch, a not-so-little natural span on the rim near the portal. Gaining access to the Poison Spider Mesa rim via the sloping strata near the portal will bypass this arch, some gigantic river-rim slickrock potholes and a good look at the sandstone fin maze across the river gorge, but will shorten the hike, if time is an element. About midway along the Poison Spider - Gold Bar rim, the large opening of Jeep Arch can be seen in a huge reddish mass of rock below the rim to the west. Getting to this large span can be a challenging side trip. Once Little Canyon is reached, it is possible to descend westward into the canyon, cross it and climb up onto its northern rim, thus gaining access to another 2 miles of rim which is a continuation of the Poison Spider - Gold Bar rim. Descent could then be via the south fork of Sevenmile Canyon to paved Utah 313, 3 miles west of U.S. 163. Hiking this additional rim-extension and leaving via Sevenmile Canyon will require at least another full day, but affords excellent views across Arches National Park to the east, a look at the rimlands and south fork of Sevenmile Canyon, and gives hikers a chance to explore some high slickrock country rarely seen by anyone.

NOTES: The Poison Spider - Gold Bar rim route is strenuous and should be attempted only by hikers in excellent physical condition.

Rainbow Rocks

TYPE OF TRAIL: slickrock.

TRAIL MILEAGE: optional, 3 to 18 miles.

TIME TO HIKE: optional, 2 hours to 2 days or more.

U.S.G.S. MAPS: The Knoll and Crescent Junction quadrangles.

HAZARDS: no water; hazardous cliffs.

SEASONS: best in early spring when desert flowers are in bloom, but may also be hiked in summer or fall.

ACCESS: Drive west on Utah 313 from U.S. 163 to Dubinky Well turnoff; drive dirt road north to unmarked road heading west a few yards south of Dubinky Well windmill; in about 2miles, this road will pass by one end of a long ridge of varicolored slickrock; leave vehicle here and ascend onto ridge via saddle about ½ mile from its end; access at other end of ridge is via the graded dirt county road that heads west from U.S. 163 just south of the Grand County airport, then an off-road vehicle trail via Levi Well and upper Tenmile Canyon.

TRAIL SUMMARY: This non-designated hiking route along a multi-colored sandstone ridge offers full-circle panoramic views of a slickrock canyon, desert washes, redrock monoliths, giant dry waterfalls and such distant scenic highlights as the San Rafael Reef, the Book Cliffs, and the La Sal and Henry Mountains.

TRAIL HIGHLIGHTS

Rainbow Rocks is a long ridge of banded Entrada sandstone topped in places by younger alluvial deposits that afford good rockhounding. One side of the ridge drops off steeply or in sheer cliffs. The other side is more terraced or rounded, or slopes into higher desert. The ridge wanders in an erratic manner across some remote but colorful and scenic desert that is seldom viewed. It is possible to leave the ridge on either side in many places, but practical access is available only at either end of the 15-mile long ridge. In addition to the outstanding near and far views afforded by hiking the ridge, hikers will encounter a wide variety of slickrock erosional forms, including potholes, deep crevices, spires, dry water falls, small natural bridges and arches, balanced rocks and rounded domes and fins. The multi-colored layering that dominates this long, continuous sandstone ridge is quite unusual in canyon country, where Entrada sandstone is generally a uniform reddish-brown in hue. Hikers will also find interesting exploring in the slickrock canyon to the north of and below the southernmost 3 miles of the Rainbow Rocks ridge. A practical one-day hike for those lacking access or egress at the northern end of the ridge would begin by parking at the southern end, with the hike going along the ridge for half a day, descending to below the ridge and returning via the cliff base and slickrock canyon.

NOTES: There is often water in potholes in one tributary of this slickrock canyon which approaches the cliff base about 2½ miles from the south end of the ridge. The water could be purified for use. The southern top of the Rainbow Rocks outcropping is called "The Needles" on U.S.G.S. topographic maps.

Spring Canyon Point

TYPE OF TRAIL: canyon rim.

TRAIL MILEAGE: optional, up to 5 miles.

TIME TO HIKE: optional, 1 hour to 1 day.

U.S.G.S. MAPS: The Knoll and Bowknot Bend quadrangles.

HAZARDS: no water; hazardous cliffs.

SEASONS: best during cooler months of spring or fall, but may also be hiked in summer or winter.

ACCESS: drive west on Utah 313 from U.S. 163 to Dubinky Well turn-off; drive dirt road north to unmarked road heading west a few yards south of Dubinky Well windmill; road soon becomes off-road vehicle trail that goes to tip of Spring Canyon Point.

TRAIL SUMMARY: Hiking the canyon rim perimeter of Spring Canyon Point affords breathtaking views down into the deep Green River gorge in the Labyrinth Canyon area, plus a close look at a wide variety of sandstone erosional forms along the rim.

TRAIL HIGHLIGHTS

Although an old vehicle trail travels the length of Spring Canyon Point, it offers views of the magnificent Green River gorge only at the tip of this slender, elevated peninsula of sandstone. Hiking the perimeter of the peninsula affords a continuous view of spectacular sheer-walled Labyrinth Canyon and the sediment-laden river that carved it from solid rock. The canyon rim is quite irregular in places, offering a challenge to hikers. At one point along the southern rim, it is possible to look across the narrow waist of Bowknot Bend, a gigantic loop in the meandering rivergorge. Views down into the gorge are exceptionally colorful from mid to late October, when the tamarisk and cottonwoods that border the river are autumn-hued, and the low water is calm and reflective. Winter views are colorful in another way, with river ice, and possibly snow in shadowed areas, accenting the reddish hues of the canyon walls. One way to spend a full day seeing the entire perimeter of Spring Canyon Point is to drive to its tip for an introductory view, retrace on the vehicle trail for 2 miles, hike to one rim or the other, then hike around the point all the way to the parked vehicle. Hikers with only highway vehicles can drive as far along the road west from Dubinky Well as practical, then walk along the vehicle trail or hike across country to the canyon rim.

NOTES: There is a small but interesting arch just a few yards to the south of the approach road, and visible from the road, somewhere beyond the gigantic mass of multi-colored sandstone called Rainbow Rocks. The southern tip of this 15-mile long outcropping is called "The Needles" on U.S.G.S. topographic maps.

Upheaval Dome

TYPE OF TRAIL: designated and primitive.

TRAIL MILEAGE: optional, ¼ to ½ mile or longer.

TIME TO HIKE: optional, ¼ to 1 hour or longer.

U.S.G.S. MAP: Upheaval Dome quadrangle, or map of Canyonlands National Park.

HAZARDS: hazardous cliffs.

SEASONS: early spring through late fall.

ACCESS: follow U.S. 163 and Utah 313 to the Knoll; where the paved road turns left to go to Dead Horse Point, continue south toward the Island in the Sky district of Canyonlands National Park; follow Park Service dirt roads and road signs to Upheaval Dome picnic site and hiking trailhead.

TRAIL SUMMARY: This short designated trail goes to viewpoints along the rim of Upheaval Dome, a spectacular, colorful and unique geological feature within Canyonlands National Park.

TRAIL HIGHLIGHTS

The trail ascends steeply from the picnic area to the elevated rim of Upheaval Dome. A short spur goes to one overlook, while a longer trail continues clockwise around the slickrock rim. The "dome" consists of an appallingly deep crater which is drained by a narrow canyon at its western end. The floor of the crater is a solid mass of colorful, sharp spires and ridges of rock which geologists indicate to be metamorphosed White Rim sandstone, a rock layer that is visible far below all the major viewpoints on Island in the Sky. The huge crater is called a "dome" because it is thought to have been formed megayears ago by upward pressure from a subterranean salt dome. Subsequent erosion has carried away the fractured rock above the harder, metamorphosed White Rim sandstone, leaving a deep crater. A Park Service brochure available at the trailhead or at various park offices explains in some detail the geology of this strange canyon country feature. For those prepared to make connections with a vehicle at the lower end, it is possible to hike down into Upheaval Dome, then out by way of Upheaval Canyon, **until the wash intersects the White Rim off-road** vehicle trail near the Green River. Check with Park Service rangers for the exact route of this rough and primitive trail, because it should not be attempted without prior registration and guidance.

NOTES: There are other short hiking trails on Island in the Sky, such as up onto Whale Rock, to Washerwoman Arch, up onto Aztec Butte and from the side road at The Neck. All of these start from Park Service roads on the Island in the Sky. For the locations of trailheads, see the Park Service brochure on Island in the Sky.

White Rim

TYPE OF TRAIL: canyon rim.

TRAIL MILEAGE: optional, up to 100 miles or more.

TIME TO HIKE: optional, 1 hour to 10 days or more.

U.S.G.S. MAPS: Hatch Point, Upheaval Dome and The Spur quadrangles, or map of Canyonlands National Park.

HAZARDS: no reliable water; hazardous cliffs.

SEASONS: best during cooler months of spring and fall, but may be hiked in summer, or winter when snow is light.

ACCESS: for access to east end of trail, drive downriver from U.S. 163 on Utah 279 to its end at the potash mill; continue on graded dirt road that climbs above the river; this road may not be passable to highway vehicles beyond potash evaporation ponds; continue on this vehicle trail to a junction at base of Shafer Trail switchbacks; follow vehicle trail signs to Musselman Arch on White Rim; for access to west end of White Rim, drive west on Utah 313 from U.S. 163 to a road sign pointing to Mineral Canyon; drive this graded dirt road to the head of the Mineral Canyon switchbacks; continue beyond canyon rim only with off-road vehicles; drive or hike down into Green River gorge, then follow downriver vehicle trail to where White Rim first appears beside river.

TRAIL SUMMARY: Hiking all or any portion of the White Rim within Canyonlands National Park affords spectacular and unique views of the looming Island in the Sky high above the rim, the great cliffs and terraced slopes of rock below the Island, the deep gorges of the Green and Colorado rivers far below and the myriad erosional forms of the White Rim itself.

TRAIL HIGHLIGHTS

Although an off-road vehicle trail gives access to the White Rim at each end, and generally follows this gigantic, irregular terrace that lies between the Island in the Sky and Green and Colorado rivers, the vehicle trail actually approaches the rim in only a few places along its 100-mile length. This leaves most of the fantastically beautiful White Rim accessible only to hikers. Hiking along this meandering rim of hard, white sandstone that is sandwiched between hundreds of feet of dark red alluvium at an intermediate level between the lofty Island in the Sky and the Green and Colorado rivers deep in their gorges, is an experience that has no parallel anywhere. The White Rim sandstone is exposed as a relatively level edge of rock that forms the upper rim of the complex system of sidecanyons to the Green and Colorado river gorges for the last few dozen miles above their confluence near the center of Canyonlands National Park. In addition to magnificent

and ever-changing views above and below the White Rim, the rim itself provides a wide range of unique features that can be found few
other places. The White Rim sandstone varies in thickness up to 250
feet. Wherever it is crossed by dry washes, the rim is undercut, forming gigantic dry waterfalls and vast caverns which often shelter
spring-fed pools and lush vegetation. Natural cracks and joints in the
White Rim erode to form immense, deep fissures, or checkerboard patterns or balanced rocks of gigantic size or fantastic shape. One
drainage line has formed Musselman Arch, which is actually a perfectly level natural bridge about 100 feet long, 6 feet wide and 4 feet thick
at its center. Hikers who closely follow the edge of the White Rim from
the vicinity of Musselman Arch to where the White Rim plunges below
the surface beside the Green River will have hiked well over 100 miles,
depending upon how many jutting points along the way have been
bypassed. It is possible, however, to break such an adventure into
shorter segments by coordinating hikes along remote stretches of the
rim with a vehicle at the various points where the rim and vehicle trail
come together. In fact, due to the lack of available water along the rim,
and the impracticality of carrying more than enough for a day or so,
such a coordinated vehicle-hiking jaunt is the only practical way to
hike most of the White Rim.

NOTES: While water is not uncommon immediately below the White
Rim, access to beneath the rim is rare. One spur of the vehicle trail will
also allow hikers access to the Colorado River down Lathrop Canyon,
and another spur goes to the Green River at the Ginpole, where early
prospectors unloaded supplies from river craft. There are also foot
routes to below the rim at Monument Basin and below Junction Butte,
but for practical backpacking purposes it is necessary for a White Rim
hiker to carry along all water needed, either on his back or in a support
vehicle.

White Wash

TYPE OF TRAIL: slickrock, sand dunes and sandy wash hiking area.

TRAIL MILEAGE: optional, 1 or more miles.

TIME TO HIKE: optional, 1 hour to several days.

U.S.G.S. MAPS: Green River and Crescent Junction quadrangles.

HAZARDS: remote location.

SEASONS: best during cooler months of spring or fall, but may be hiked in summer, or winter when snow does not close access road.

ACCESS: from the south, drive north on U.S. 163 to county dirt road that goes west just south of county airport; go west on this road until it ends at Floy Wash road; drive southwestward on Floy Wash road for about 7½ miles to an oil-pumping station; White Wash is the area visible to the southeast below ridge the road is following; a dirt road just beyond pumping installation goes down into White Wash; from east or west; turn off of U.S. 6 & 50 onto Floy Wash road; there may not be an interchange at this road from Interstate 70; WARNING — the county dirt roads that provide access to White Wash are generally impassable during and following rain, and are very poorly maintained, making them hazardous to standard highway vehicles.

TRAIL SUMMARY: White Wash contains one of the largest areas of "living" sand dunes in canyon country, together with a branching wash system, perennial springs, and gigantic masses of eroded sandstone slickrock, a combination that has produced a beautiful and unique hiking area.

TRAIL HIGHLIGHTS

At first glance, White Wash may look like countless other drywashes in canyon country, yet further examination reveals that it is different in several ways. The wash, as first seen from the access road, is surrounded by hundreds of acres of salmon-pink sand dunes that darken in color as they near huge domes and ridges of red-hued Entrada sandstone. The broad wash is white sand, but bordered by water-loving vegetation, revealing that the wash sand is perennially wet just below the surface. Healthy cottonwood trees growing among the shifting sand dunes also tell of sub-surface moisture. Some of the upper branches of the wash, as they meander endlessly among giant dunes and great walls of slickrock, are dry. Others contain reflective pools of spring water that is potable if purified. One spring even has a small marshy area, where water-loving plants grow in profusion. At one place along the main wash, spring water trickles from between big sand dunes, only to sink out of sight in the dryer wash sand. The water sources in upper White Wash make the area an excellent place to camp, but only hikers or off-road vehicles should attempt to reach the springs. There are no special hiking routes within White Wash. Hikers can select routes to suit their interests from the variety of washbottom, slickrock and dune hiking available. Each of these has its own special aesthetic highlights. The wash has its springs and system of winding, dead-end canyons to explore. The sand dunes exhibit an endless variety of shape and, in early spring contain an amazing diversity of desert wildflowers. Some of the shrubby perennials there blossom in the late summer and fall. The slickrock offers hikers a close look at several varieties of tenacious desert plant life, big potholes that often contain water, small caves, crevices, ledges and colorful panoramic views from high points. The lower wash, as it heads toward the Green River 3 miles away, contains millions of pieces of colorful agate and other minerals from higher surrounding strata. The newer rock layers above the upper wash also provide good rockhounding. Taken altogether, White Wash offers a hiking area of unique natural beauty and variety.

NOTES: On rare occasions, generally on weekends, the White Wash dunes may be used by a few local sandbuggy fans. This may detract somewhat from the solitude of the area, but in compensation will afford hikers some novel entertainment, because White Wash sand dunes contain areas of dry "quicksand" that can trap unwary buggies.

Survival

It was mid-August, the hottest time of the year in canyon country. I was riding with two friends, a man and his wife, in their four wheel drive pickup, showing them a vehicle trail route through a remote desert-drywash region.

The laboring truck dipped steeply downward to cross a rocky wash. As it pointed its hood skyward to climb back out, its wheels plowed deeply into soft, dry sand, killing its laboring engine. The driver let the truck roll backward until it was level, then tried to start the engine. A short groan, then a few feeble clacks, then nothing. A bad electrical connection? A bum starter? A dead battery? No way to start the truck by pushing — it was at the bottom of a narrow, rough wash.

The vehicle's owner worked doggedly on the truck in the blazing heat, while his wife and I huddled in the sparse shade of a big, overhanging bush. No luck. We paused for a glum lunch, cherishing the liquids we had as the temperature climbed to 105, 110, maybe higher in that stifling wash.

More mechanical work. No results. We held a council of war. It was at least 6 miles to the nearest back country dirt road, then another 9 to the highway, with very small chance of anyone traveling the dirt road. Fifteen blazing-hot miles, along a sandy, dusty trail and road.

I advised waiting with the truck. We had a little food left from lunch, a canteen of water, a six-pack of beer and a little ice in the cooler. My wife knew roughly where we were going, and would initiate a search. We had long since agreed to a plan for such emergencies, and had firmly instructed our daughter and friends in its simple details.

Our plan was this: before heading into canyon country by vehicle or on foot, we told someone our probable route and return time. If we did not return as scheduled, they were to report to the authorities, but start no search until the next day.

But my friends had left their young children with a babysitter, so he decided to walk out. His wife, worried over my admonitions, decided to go along, although her shoes were no good for desert hiking. I felt better about the two of them together.

I gave them all the water and part of the beer. They left me the ice, left-over lunch and two cans of beer, then headed out across the blazing-hot desert. I hugged the sparse shade, worrying about them for a few minutes, then started searching my memory, studying the vague image there of a topographic map, trying to orient myself with something I had seen on my only other trip through this region.

It just had to be somewhere not far ahead. I stuck a can of beer in my pocket and started off in the heat, following the vehicle trail toward the shimmering rock-and-sand horizon, deliberately leaving plenty of obvious foot tracks.

Within a quarter mile I knew I was right. Within another hot mile the trail dropped into a broad sandy wash with a big, shady grove of cottonwoods, trees that only grow where they can get their roots into reliable moisture. A high dirt embankment walled the wash on the far side, and a solid rock cliff loomed above that.

And there, in a verdant patch at the base of that cliff stood a short ladder. Above the ladder, a big bucket hung from a steel peg. Strips of mossy sheet metal wired to other pegs caught dripping moisture and channeled it into the bucket. And an ordinary faucet had been tarred into a hole in the bucket's bottom edge.

Water! Sweet, cool water!

And still better, my memory reminded me, there was an old cowboy line shack just beyond the wash, but still out of sight.

I climbed to the dripping spring, ascended the ladder and opened the faucet barely enough to let me splash my hot head and drink a few sips of that welcome desert nectar. I then headed for the line shack. Its door was hooked against desert winds, but unlocked, a surviving remnant of early-west tradition.

I spent the long afternoon on the shady porch of that line shack, reading a Reader's Digest that should have been in a museum, and taking an occasional walk to the spring. Toward evening, I returned the thoroughly-read magazine to its dusty shelf, closed the shack door tightly and headed back toward the stranded truck by the last rays of sunlight, sipping the beer I had brought as I walked.

The desert sunset was lovely as I sat on a rock outcropping near the truck, slowly savoring the leftover lunch and sipping the last beer. After dark, I planned to walk back to the cabin by starlight, to spend the warm desert night on one of its dusty but serviceable bunks. The desert dusk was beautiful, and I was at peace with the world.

I was actually disappointed when headlights appeared, bobbing across the darkening desert before I had even finished my scanty meal. Rescued—but too soon, too soon!

I was relieved, however, to know that my friends had survived their arduous trek. As luck had it, they had been picked up only a short time after reaching that rarely-traveled dirt road, with nothing but a strong thirst and a few footblisters to show for their hazardous desert hike.

But by knowing that desert's secrets, I had survived in style and comfort—sitting on the shady porch of an old cattleman's shack and sipping the cool water from his precious spring. And silently thanking that unknown pioneer for his old-west hospitality.

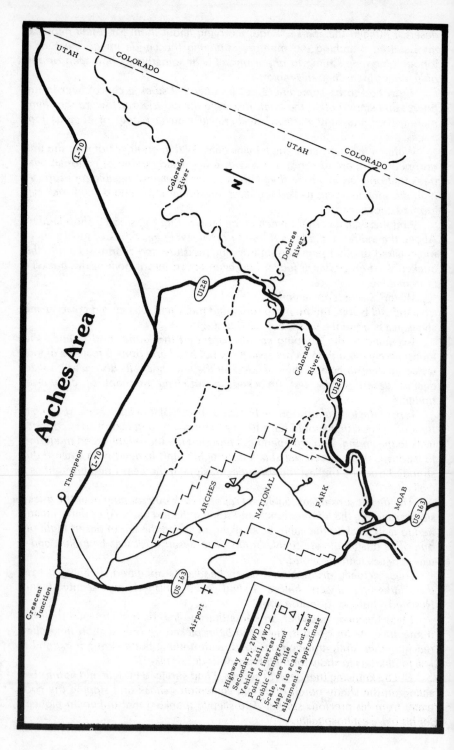

Arches Area

UTAH   COLORADO

UTAH   COLORADO

I-70

Colorado River

N

Dolores River

UI28

Colorado River

UI28

Thompson

I-70

ARCHES   NATIONAL   PARK

MOAB

US 163

Crescent Junction

US 163

Airport

Highway
Secondary, 2WD
Vehicle trail, 4WD
Point of interest
Public campground
Scale, one mile
Map is to scale, but road
alignment is approximate

Arches Area

AREA NAME: This area was named after Arches National Park which occupies the southern end of the area.

AREA BOUNDARIES: Interstate 70, U.S. 163, Colorado River, Utah-Colorado border.

U.S.G.S. TOPOGRAPHIC MAPS THAT COVER THE AREA: Moab, Castle Valley, Cisco, Coates Creek, Thompson, Crescent Junction; a 25" by 34" map of Arches National Park and vicinity also covers part of this area.

GENERAL TOPOGRAPHY: high, rolling desert bordered by deep canyon systems along both southern boundaries; slashed by many sidecanyons along the Colorado River gorge; gigantic ridges and areas of slickrock domes and fins dominate Arches National Park and vicinity.

SUGGESTED BASE CAMPS: motels or commercial campgrounds in Moab; developed public campground in Arches National Park; primitive camping is permitted almost anywhere within the area except within Arches National Park; contact park rangers for current regulations there.

ACCESS ROUTES: Interstate 70, U.S. 163, Utah 128, county roads and off-road vehicle trails as shown on the area map.

AREA NOTES:
1.   The non-designated hiking trails, routes and areas listed are just representative samples of the primitive hiking available in this area.
2.   The geologic formations exposed in this area to the north, east and west of Arches National Park provide excellent rockhounding.
3.   The large area to the northeast of the park contains many old uranium mines and off-road vehicle trails, but also has many unspoiled canyons worth exploring on foot. Most of this area is so primitive, remote and inaccessible, except by off-road vehicle, that hiking there is impractical except from such a support vehicle.

Hum - m - m - m

Three in our small hiking group were sitting on a horizontal limb of a gnarled old juniper tree beside the trail, resting a bit and admiring the graceful, unbelievable expanse of Landscape Arch. The air was calm, the day warm. For several minutes we talked intermittently in subdued tones, distracted, bemused by the awesome beauty of this widest natural span in the country, perhaps the whole world.

Then my sister, who was sitting beside me on that juniper limb said, "What's that funny sound?" We all sat quietly and listened. There was a faint, dry rustling and a low buzz of sound coming from somewhere. I turned my head this way and that, seeking the source of the odd sounds. After several baffled seconds I looked closer, much closer. And focused on a small swarm of bees clinging in a tight ball to the limb we were sitting on, just a couple of feet away.

Our movements on the limb had slightly disturbed this swarm of bees, which was fortunately in a quiescent stage, eliciting the sounds we had heard — the rustling of thousands of tiny feet and wings in the swarm, and the faint buzz of the few who were in close orbit around the cluster.

Our fatigue suddenly, magically relieved, we slowly, carefully got up from the limb we had been sharing with the swarm, and slowly, peacefully left that tree to our pack of humming little friends. Hopefully, they later found a more congenial place to build a new hive for their transient young queen.

58

Courthouse Wash

TYPE OF TRAIL: canyon-stream.

TRAIL MILEAGE: optional, 5 to 15 miles.

TIME TO HIKE: optional, ½ to 2 days.

U.S.G.S. MAPS: Moab quadrangle, or map of Arches National Park.

HAZARDS: mosquitoes in lower 2 miles during warmer months.

SEASONS: best during spring or late fall months, but may be hiked in summer, or winter when snow is light.

ACCESS: to hike full length of wash, drive 12 miles north from Colorado River bridge on U.S. 163 to where Courthouse Wash closely parallels the highway; to enter wash midway, drive 8 miles north from Colorado River bridge on U.S. 163 to where highway crosses Sevenmile wash, then hike down this to Courthouse; to hike only lower wash, enter Arches National Park from U.S. 163, 2 miles north of Colorado River bridge, drive to Courthouse Towers area of park and hike down Courthouse Wash from where road crosses it, about 5 miles from park entrance; alternately, hike up wash from where U.S. 163 crosses it ¼ mile north of Colorado River bridge.

TRAIL SUMMARY: Courthouse Wash offers hikers a beautiful and varied route, from open desert wash to narrow watered gorge to broad red-walled canyon to deep and narrow redrock gorge, with most of the hike within Arches National Park.

TRAIL HIGHLIGHTS

For the first 6 miles east of U.S. 163, Courthouse Wash is a typical desert drywash crossing arid, open land. This is relieved for the first 2 miles by low hills of colorful "painted desert" Morrison deposits which provide fine rockhounding fairly close to the wash. Shortly after the wash enters Arches National Park, it drops abruptly down a rock ledge and flowing springs create a perennial stream that steadily gains in flow for the next several miles before disappearing beneath the sandy canyon floor for 3 or 4 miles, then to reappear where the canyon narrows and deepens for the last 5 miles. From where the stream starts, it cuts sharply into solid rock, forming a narrow, verdant canyon that gradually deepens and widens on its twisting journey toward the Courthouse Towers section of Arches. In many places, springs dripping from the walls of this enchanting linear oasis create lush hanging gardens of water-loving plants. Some of the larger springs have slowly formed huge alcoves in the soaring redrock canyon walls. A few of these contain crystal-clear pools of delicious water. One such gigantic alcove called "Sleepy Hollow" has a pool large enough for swimming, but is not easy to locate because it is hidden behind masses of trees and other vegetation. As the flowing stream sinks below the sandy canyon

floor, the canyon broadens and is walled by great convoluted masses of eroded, salmon-hued Entrada sandstone. Where the wash crosses the more open country in the Courthouse Towers area, the colorful cliffs recede, or form massive, free-standing towers or slabs of rock reminiscent of familiar shapes. Some of these bear names, such as the Three Gossips, The Organ, Sheep Rock and the Tower of Babel. Soon after the wash goes under the paved park road, it cuts quickly into rock strata, becoming once again a deep, narrow and spectacular gorge with trickling stream, pools and echoing alcoves. The 6 mile stretch between the park road and where Courthouse Wash reaches U.S. 163 and the Colorado River is a favorite, but warm-weather hikers are warned to go well prepared for mosquitoes. One delightful alternate to hiking the arid upper 6 miles of Courthouse Wash before entering the park is to hike down lower Sevenmile Canyon, beginning where U.S. 163 crosses it 8 miles north of the Colorado River bridge. After a few hundred yards this shallow, open wash plunges over a breathtaking dry waterfall to become a deep, lovely and unspoiled canyon. An old stock trail gives access to the canyon floor a short distance to the right of the dry waterfall. This trail can be seen from the drop-off. Lower Sevenmile Canyon joins Courthouse Wash after about 3 miles, but hikers who do not want to miss one of the loveliest stretches of Courthouse should hike up that canyon from the Sevenmile confluence for at least 2 miles before heading back down-canyon.

NOTES: Hikers who plan to travel the two wet stretches of Courthouse Wash should be prepared to wade frequently. Most of the spring water in the central stretches of Courthouse can be considered potable without purification for hikers who plan overnight camping along the way. There is an easy 1 mile foot trail within the Courthouse Towers area that goes through Park Avenue between roadside turnouts.

Delicate Arch

TYPE OF TRAIL: designated.

TRAIL MILEAGE: 3 miles round trip.

TIME TO HIKE: 2 to 4 hours.

U.S.G.S. MAPS: Moab and Castle Valley quadrangles, or map of Arches National Park.

HAZARDS: half of trail is steep and very hot during warmer months; no water; hazardous cliff behind Delicate Arch.

SEASONS: best during cooler months of spring or fall, but may be hiked in summer, or winter when snow is not too deep.

ACCESS: drive into Arches National Park from U.S. 163, 2 miles north of the Colorado River bridge; stay on main park road to Delicate Arch side road; Delicate Arch trailhead is at Wolfe Ranch parking area 1½ miles from turnoff.

TRAIL SUMMARY: This short but popular trail goes through a colorful, mineralized area, climbs a steep slickrock slope, then continues up a sand-and-rock gulch to Delicate Arch, thought by many to be the most picturesque of the numerous arches within this national park.

TRAIL HIGHLIGHTS

The Delicate Arch trail begins at Wolfe Ranch, where an old log cabin and other pioneer structures and artifacts represent a pre-park segment of Arches history. The trail then crosses upper Salt Wash on a footbridge, winds through low, colorful outcroppings of minerals then climbs a steep slickrock slope. At the top of this slope, the trail continues up an eroded sandstone gully that is studded with pinyon and juniper trees and other hardy desert vegetation. As the trail crosses a steep rock slope, it goes beneath a "window" in the sandstone wall to the right of the trail. A peek through that natural window will afford a first dramatic glimpse of Delicate Arch. A few yards farther on, the designated trail ends at an overlook quite near the arch. With care, it is possible to walk around the large, steep-walled natural bowl that lies between the overlook and Delicate Arch. This short walk affords still other picturesque angles and backgrounds for viewing or photographing this unusual span. Although Delicate Arch "steals the show" on this trail, there is another fairly large arch nearby that is visible from the hiking trail.

NOTES: Although it is possible to climb around Delicate Arch on the south side, this is very hazardous. Hikers wanting a somewhat safer view of the arch from the south can hike out onto a point of rock there, but should be wary of the sheer cliffs along this point. The most dramatic lighting on Delicate Arch for photography is late afternoon, near sunset.

Double-O Arch

TYPE OF TRAIL: designated.

TRAIL MILEAGE: about 5 miles round trip, plus optional short spur trails to various arches.

TIME TO HIKE: 3 to 5 hours.

U.S.G.S. MAPS: Thompson quadrangle, or map of Arches National Park.

HAZARDS: hazardous drops in a few places; no water.

SEASONS: best during cooler months of spring or fall, but may be hiked in summer.

ACCESS: drive into Arches National Park from U.S. 163, 2 miles north of the Colorado River bridge; stay on main park road to its end in Devils Garden area; trailhead is here.

TRAIL SUMMARY: This loop trail with several short spurs takes hikers through a fantastically varied array of sandstone formations to several large natural arches, one of them the widest known span in the country, another an over-under double arch.

TRAIL HIGHLIGHTS

This fascinating trail immediately enters a group of towering sandstone fins. The first mile of the trail, to famous Landscape Arch, the widest known span, is an easy trail that has been surfaced. Beyond Landscape, the trail is more primitive and goes through a maze of spectacular, weathered, sandstone outcroppings. Along the way, short side trails lead to various interesting arches, such as Tunnel Arch, Pinetree Arch, Partition Arch, Navajo Arch, and Black Arch. Along one stretch, the trail travels the tops of a series of slickrock fins, offering views down into a maze of similar fins. One short trail spur goes to a viewpoint which provides a look down Fin Canyon, with its radiating rows of gigantic parallel sandstone fins, and Black Arch, a great hole through one of these fins. At 2 miles, the trail reaches Double-O Arch, a large round opening over a smaller one, both through the same gracefully arching sandstone fin. An age-blackened sandstone pinnacle called the Dark Angel is visible to the north from this vicinity. The trail beyond Double-O is relatively new and is marked by stone cairns at intervals. The new stretch of trail starts through the lower opening of Double-O Arch, then angles downward through the sandstone fin maze that borders Fin Canyon and its tributaries. The trail is highly picturesque, and even awe-inspiring in places where it travels between soaring, age-patinaed red slickrock walls hundreds of feet high and only yards apart. One short side trip along this stretch that should not be missed leaves the designated trail where it drops into the sandy wash-bottom of Fin Canyon. There, hikers should walk upwash for a few yards, then turn left into a small side wash choked with brush and trees which goes into a spectacular grotto between two great rock fins, one of them containing the large opening that is Black Arch. The size and shape of this awe-inspiring grotto, and the lighting effects there from afternoon on to sunset, provide a highlight along this trail. The balance of this loop trail continues through beautiful sand and slickrock country to rejoin the main trail at Landscape Arch.

NOTES: While the hike to Landscape Arch is quite easy, the trail loop that goes beyond this arch is much more primitive and demanding. The Park Service has available a useful trail guide for this loop hike.

Dry Mesa

TYPE OF TRAIL: canyon rim.

TRAIL MILEAGE: optional, up to 20 miles.

U.S.G.S. MAPS: Moab and Castle Valley quadrangles.

HAZARDS: no water; hazardous cliffs.

SEASONS: best during cooler months of spring or fall, but may be hiked in summer.

ACCESS: drive into Arches National Park from U.S. 163, 2 miles north of Colorado River bridge; stay on main park road to Delicate Arch side road; drive toward Wolfe Ranch parking area, but follow road fork right toward Delicate Arch viewpoint; just before this viewpoint, take unmarked four wheel drive trail to right up Cache Valley; drive or hike this trail up onto Dry Mesa.

TRAIL SUMMARY: This desert wilderness hiking route follows the rim of a high, isolated mesa that lies just outside of Arches National Park and affords breathtaking views down into Salt Wash, the Colorado River gorge and Cache Valley, the three deep and spectacular gorges that isolate the mesa.

TRAIL HIGHLIGHTS

For those without four-wheel vehicles, it is possible to park at the Delicate Arch viewpoint then follow the off-road vehicle trail up colorful Cache Valley, then up onto Dry Mesa. Those who have four wheel drive vehicles may choose to drive up onto the mesa, then leave the seldom-used vehicle trail for a hike around all or part of the mesa rim. Cache Valley is a jumble of colorful sedimentary rock strata and outcroppings, with unusual sandstone spires at its eastern end, as well as interesting canyon-washes and an old mine cave. While hikers can climb up onto Dry Mesa many places along Cache Valley, it is worth staying in the valley to its upper end in order to see those highlights. On top of the mesa, the vehicle trail makes a rough loop, with joggings made by early seismograph crews, but hikers who want to see all the mesa route has to offer should stay close to the mesa rim all the way around, deviating only when forced to by tributary canyons. A counter-clockwise route will give hikers chromatic views back down into Cache Valley and the wild country to the north, and fascinating glimpses down into the red-walled maze of lower Salt Wash and beyond into the Windows Section of Arches National Park. Along the southern rim of the mesa, the spectacular, sheer-walled Colorado River gorge dominates the route. Perhaps the most colorful part of the whole rim route is at the eastern tip of the mesa, where a short spur of the river gorge cuts into the cliffs to meet upper Cache Valley. There, an area of tortured, eroded, pastel-hued rock and mesa-top sand dunes offers hikers a view that seems almost unearthly.

NOTES: While it is possible for hikers to get down to the Colorado River from the east end of Dry Mesa, or via Salt Wash, it is then not possible to get across the river, and it is quite dangerous and difficult to try going down the north river bank to U.S. 163. Hikers are advised to approach and leave Dry Mesa by way of Cache Valley and the road to Delicate Arch.

Fiery Furnace

TYPE OF TRAIL: designated and guided.

TRAIL MILEAGE: 1¼ miles.

TIME TO HIKE: about 1 hour.

U.S.G.S. MAPS: Moab and Thompson quadrangles, or map of Arches National Park.

HAZARDS: trail must be taken with Park Service guide to avoid getting lost.

SEASONS: good any time from early spring through late fall; closed during winter.

ACCESS: drive into Arches National Park from U.S. 163, 2 miles north of Colorado River bridge; stay on main park road to Fiery Furnace spur road; trail starts at parking area at end of spur.

TRAIL SUMMARY: This short but extremely beautiful and unusual hiking trail winds through a maze of tall, rust-colored sandstone fins and spires, with dry waterfalls, pools, arches and natural bridges along the way.

TRAIL HIGHLIGHTS

Because of the labyrinthine nature of the Fiery Furnace area of Arches, it is necessary for hikers to accompany a knowledgeable Park Service guide. A schedule of guided hikes is available at the park visitor center. The trail leaves the Fiery Furnace parking area and wends its way through rock outcroppings and drywashes to the Fiery Furnace, where a locked gate bars unguided access. There is a similar gate at the egress end of the trail. Between the gates, the trail goes up narrow washes and crevices between sandstone fins hundreds of feet high, through echoing slickrock grottoes, along elevated ledges and between close rock walls, with the entire hike dominated by lofty, needle-like pinnacles set within narrow slits of blue sky. One short side trail goes to an unusual arch with a double opening. The Fiery Furnace was so named because of the bright fiery glare of sunlight reflected from the reddish-colored rock when the sun is high.

NOTES: Photographers who want to capture the awe-inspiring majesty of the Fiery Furnace should take along wide angle lenses. Hikers should not attempt to enter any part of the huge Fiery Furnace area unguided, because the danger of getting lost in this complex maze is very real. Even highly developed trail-reading skills are of limited value with the sand and slickrock that dominate this geologic oddity.

Klondike Bluffs

TYPE OF TRAIL: slickrock and sand, plus short designated trail.

TRAIL MILEAGE: optional, 2 miles or more.

TIME TO HIKE: optional, 2 hours to 2 days or more.

U.S.G.S. MAPS: Thompson quadrangle, or map of Arches National Park.

HAZARDS: no water; dangerous drops.

SEASONS: best during cooler months of spring or fall, but may be hiked in summer, or winter when snow is light.

ACCESS: two obscure off-road vehicle trails from Little Valley to the west of Arches National Park give access to the Klondike Bluffs area of the park; more practical access is via park roads and trails; drive onto Arches National Park from U.S. 163, 2 miles north of Colorado River bridge; stay on main park road to turnoff onto a dirt road near Skyline Arch that enters Salt Valley; stay on this road to Klondike Bluffs-Tower Arch turnoff; drive 1 mile to parking area and hiking trailhead to Tower Arch; hike to Tower Arch, which is within Klondike Bluffs.

TRAIL SUMMARY: Hiking within the Klondike Bluffs area is much like hiking through the Fiery Furnace, except that the gigantic sandstone fins and towers are somewhat more open, a Park Service guide is not required and the only designated trail is the one to Tower Arch.

TRAIL HIGHLIGHTS

The Klondike Bluffs area in the northwest corner of Arches National Park is visible for miles from U.S. 163 as an immense upthrust of white-topped, reddish rock that slopes upward to the east and is eroded along cracks and joints to form great ridges, fins and towers. Gigantic Tower Arch is below one such white-capped tower, but is only visible from nearby. Park roads and a 1-mile foot trail go to Tower Arch, but for adventurous hikers, this is just the beginning, because this picturesque natural span is surrounded on all sides by a square mile or more of fascinatingly beautiful and complex sandstone erosion forms. Slender, towering fins, balanced rocks, wind-polished spires, echoing grottoes and still other arches are set among sandy washes, salmon-hued dunes and tenacious desert trees and plant-life. It is possible to spend hours or even days exploring this intricate, colorful sandstone labyrinth. Near the northern end of the Klondike Bluffs area, there are ways to climb up onto the white sandstone caprock of this formation, and from there follow a lofty eroded ridge that protrudes back southward into the redrock area. This high promontory affords a spectacular, full-circle panoramic view of Arches National Park, the La Sal Mountains to the south, the Book Cliffs to the north, the Uncompahgre Plateau to the east and a vast array of complex canyon country in the near distance in all directions.

NOTES: This same promontory in the Klondike Bluffs can be reached by an off-road vehicle trail shown on a locally available "jeep trail map." Although the trail is difficult to find and follow, it is possible with careful use of the trail map, together with the Moab and Thompson topographic quadrangles, to reach the promontory, which could then be used as a base from which to explore the Klondike Bluffs on foot.

Squaw Park

TYPE OF TRAIL: canyon rim.

TRAIL MILEAGE: optional, up to 25 miles round trip, or more.

TIME TO HIKE: optional, up to 4 days or more.

U.S.G.S. MAPS: Cisco quadrangle.

HAZARDS: no potable water; hazardous cliffs.

SEASONS: best during cooler months of spring or fall, but may be hiked in summer, or winter when snow is light.

ACCESS: turn onto Utah 128 from U.S. 163 at south end of Colorado River bridge; drive upriver to Dewey Bridge, where Utah 128 crosses river; cross bridge and continue on for about 1mile; park and climb up onto east end of slickrock bluff that is visible north of Dewey Bridge.

TRAIL SUMMARY: Hiking along the top of the winding slickrock bluff that marks the northern wall of a huge and beautiful primitive area called Squaw Park affords colorful panoramic views, excellent rockhounding and access to several arches, old uranium mines, giant caves, seeping springs and a vast area of seldom-seen desert canyons.

TRAIL HIGHLIGHTS

There is a banded, convoluted wall of colorful Entrada sandstone that begins not far east of Arches National Park, twists generally eastward through primitive desert-canyon country for miles to discontinue briefly at the Colorado River. It then resumes again, roughly parallel to the Dolores River for many miles, before also leaping that rugged gorge to continue for many more miles on into the state of Colorado. Natural erosional processes have cut many discontinuities in this massive wall in addition to the two river gorges. Attaining the summit of any of the various sections of this great wall and hiking along its top can be very challenging and rewarding. This is especially true of the fairly continuous stretch from Dewey Bridge west toward Arches. As the top of the sandstone bluff is first reached, the small valley and ranches beside the river near Dewey Bridge are spread out below. Within about 2½ miles, a ridge that protrudes from the bluff terminates on a group of picturesque spires. Along the next several miles, old mine trails cross the bluff top and angle down toward long-abandoned uranium mines. At about ridge-mile 3 from the river, there is an unusual window-type arch opening high in the wall of a gigantic cliff-base alcove. One mile beyond this, an arch with an arrowhead-shaped opening connects two domes on a slickrock ridge that extends from the main bluff. Another window-arch opening is high in the cliff about ½ mile farther west. Several circuitous miles farther along the sandstone bluff, after three major discontinuities in its gracefully eroded contours, another fairly straight stretch of wall has a series of caves in its base. One of these caves has a number of old historic inscriptions on its walls, including a few prehistoric petroglyphs. All of these should be left undisturbed, with no modern additions that would detract from their historic value. The bluff-top hiking route can be stopped and retraced almost anywhere, but perhaps the most rewarding and varied hike in this area would be a 3- or 4-day jaunt that would roughly follow the bluff top to a point well west of the series of caves, which are shown on the Cisco topographic quadrangle, then descend to return eastward along the base of the bluff, for a close look at the caves, arches and giant alcoves, and perhaps to explore some of the many fascinating tributary canyons in the Squaw Park lowlands.

NOTES: While there are spring-fed pools of water in the cliff-base caves, and elsewhere in Squaw Park, hikers should not rely upon these for drinking water as they are contaminated by domestic livestock. Hikers should also take note that hiking this primitive bluff-top and bluff-base route is not straight, easy walking, and thus requires considerably more time and strength than normal for the mileages involved.

Windows

TYPE OF TRAIL: designated.

TRAIL MILEAGE: optional, up to 1 mile.

TIME TO HIKE: optional, up to 2 hours.

U.S.G.S. MAPS: Moab quadrangle, or map of Arches National Park.

HAZARDS: hazardous drops behind Double Arch and North Window.

SEASONS: excellent any season.

ACCESS: drive into Arches National Park from U.S. 163, 2 miles north of Colorado River bridge; stay on main park road to Windows Section side road just beyond Balanced Rock pull-off; park at end-of-road loop; trailheads are here.

TRAIL SUMMARY: Two short designated trails go to Double Arch, Turret Arch, the North and South Windows and several lesser spans in this picturesque section of Arches National Park.

TRAIL HIGHLIGHTS

The short foot trails in this developed section of Arches National Park offer few challenges to the backcountry hiker, but are nonetheless well worth taking by anyone wishing to become familiar with the unique natural beauty to be found in this park. The Windows Section of the park consists of completely eroded masses of rust-colored Entrada sandstone exposed in one of the higher areas in the park. The sandstone has weathered over eons of time into huge, rounded domes, fins and a great variety of spires, ridges, arches, windows and balanced rocks. The paved spur road ends within a large amphitheater in this colorful mass of rock, and short foot trails go to Turret Arch and the North and South Windows in one direction, and to beautiful Double Arch in the other.

NOTES: Some hikers may choose to go beyond the designated trails for more intimate looks at these natural spans and the picturesque vicinity. Climbing up into the rock openings provides interesting views and photographic angles.

" . . . And Not a Drop to Drink"

Several of us were poking around at an old copper mining site we had come across in the terribly distorted desertlands to the northwest of Arches National Park. The collapsed remains of very old equipment designed to extract copper metal from its ore lay about, long since stiffened into its final rigor mortis by thick rust at every pivot and joint. A dynamite-blasted segment of nearby cliff, still showing traces of pale green coloration, indicated the source of the copper ore.

As I walked around, looking at discarded boots so old their leather was like stone, studying what remained of huge piles of the crushed tin cans that had been used in the extraction process, I marveled at how much work a rainbow-chasing miner will do for so little return. The mine had obviously been a bust.

I stopped, my attention drawn by a slight rise in the sandy ground. An old concrete block sat on top of that inconspicuous hump. My curiosity aroused, I moved the block and found what I had expected—a neat, round 5-inch hole drilled straight down into solid sandstone.

As I had done countless times before with such drill holes, I dropped a pebble into the hole to sound its depth. Most holes I had found were not deep at all—either not deep to begin with, or long since collapsed.

Unbelieving, I dropped in a second pebble and this time counted. Incredible!

I called over the others, to share with them my wondrous hole. As we all stood quietly, attentively around that little round eye-in-the-rock, I ceremoniously dropped still another chert pebble into its depths. Silently, each person counted the seconds as the pebble rattled down and down and down—21, 22, 23—a long second's pause, then SPLASH!

A drill hole, how deep? It would take a physicist to calculate, what with friction, air resistance, free-fall formulas and the like. But deep, very deep, and solid rock all the way down. We could tell this by the echoing rattle that was clearly audible the entire time. Then the silent pause, which had to mean a big cavern, followed by a deep-water splash.

A whole underground cave full of water! Perhaps an underground lake in the perpetual darkness of a gigantic sandstone cavern, directly below this bone-dry desert. All that water there, so near—"But not a drop to drink," to borrow an old sailor's lament.

71

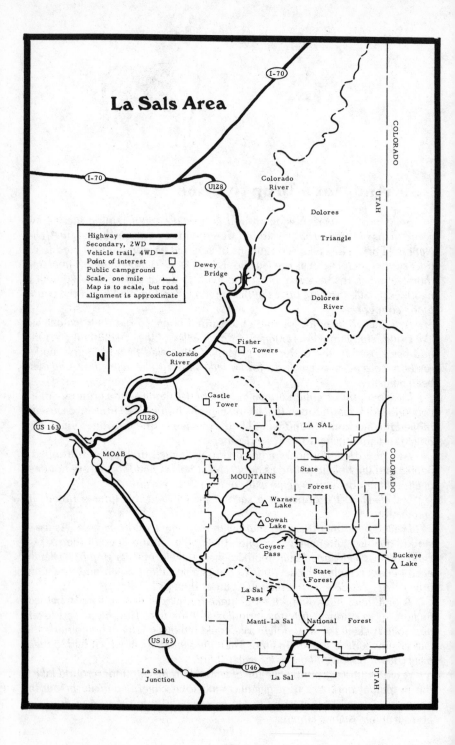

La Sals Area

Highway
Secondary, 2WD
Vehicle trail, 4WD
Point of interest □
Public campground △
Scale, one mile
Map is to scale, but road
alignment is approximate

I-70
U128
Colorado River
Dolores Triangle
Dewey Bridge
Dolores River
Fisher Towers □
Colorado River
N
Castle Tower □
LA SAL
US 163
U128
MOAB
MOUNTAINS
State Forest
Warner Lake △
Oowah Lake △
Geyser Pass
Buckeye Lake △
State Forest
La Sal Pass
Manti-La Sal National Forest
US 163
U46
La Sal Junction
La Sal
COLORADO
UTAH
COLORADO
UTAH

72

La Sals Area

AREA NAME: This area was named after the La Sal Mountains that dominate the area.

AREA BOUNDARIES: Colorado River, U.S. 163, Utah 46, Utah-Colorado border.

U.S.G.S. TOPOGRAPHIC MAPS THAT COVER THE AREA: Moab, Castle Valley, Cisco, Coates Creek, Polar Mesa, La Sal Junction, and La Sal quadrangles.

GENERAL TOPOGRAPHY: high, wooded mountains, foothill areas of sloping, wooded highlands slashed by spectacular canyons and gorges, especially to the east, north and west of the mountains; non-mountainous canyon country in the "Dolores Triangle" area formed by the Dolores and Colorado rivers and the Utah-Colorado border.

SUGGESTED BASE CAMPS: motels or commercial campgrounds in Moab; developed public campgrounds at Warner Lake, Oowah Lake and Buckeye Reservoir; limited camping is permitted at picnic sites and natural areas beside the Colorado River along Utah 128; primitive camping is permitted almost anywhere within the area except on private land, which is generally posted.

ACCESS ROUTES: U.S. 163, Utah 128, Utah 46, county roads, Forest Service roads and off-road vehicle trails as shown on the area map.

AREA NOTES:
1. The non-designated hiking trails, routes and areas listed are just representative samples of the primitive hiking available in this area.
2. There is no reliable, practical vehicular access into the Dolores Triangle area. This primitive area is penetrated by a few county roads and off-road vehicle trails from Colorado, or can be entered from Utah by fording the Dolores River when water flow is low enough to make this practical, but due to its relative inaccessibility, the Dolores Triangle area is not covered in this book.
3. The U.S. Forest Service sells two maps of the La Sal Mountains area. One is small, the other much larger. Both may be obtained at the Forest Service office at 446 South Main in Moab. The smaller map is useful only for the alignment of the major roads in the mountains and general vicinity. The larger map is more detailed, but of very limited value to hikers because it does not show surface contours.

Beaver Creek

TYPE OF TRAIL: canyon-stream.

TRAIL MILEAGE: optional, up to 18 miles or more.

TIME TO HIKE: optional, up to 3 days or more.

U.S.G.S. MAPS: Polar Mesa quadrangle.

HAZARDS: primitive, very remote mountainous and canyon country.

SEASONS: higher stretches accessible only during summer and fall; lower stretches best during cooler months of spring or fall, but may be hiked in summer, or winter when snow is light.

ACCESS: for access at Beaver Creek headwaters, drive upriver from U.S. 163 on Utah 128 to Castle Valley turn-off; drive up Castle Valley to end of paved road; continue on graded dirt Castleton-Gateway Forest Service road to Beaver Basin turn-off; hike or drive this off-road vehicle trail to Beaver Basin, where Beaver Creek begins; for access at one intermediate point on creek, continue toward Gateway on Castleton-Gateway road for about 1 mile beyond turn-off to Beaver Basin, where road crosses Beaver Creek; for access or egress at lower end of Beaver Creek canyon, drive to Gateway, Colorado, continue down west side of Dolores River on graded dirt county road to Beaver Creek, about 10 miles from Gateway.

TRAIL SUMMARY: Beaver Creek is a long mountain stream that travels from a high, wooded valley in the northeastern La Sal Mountains, through forested highlands to go the length of an unspoiled picturesque redrock canyon that ends at the Dolores River gorge.

TRAIL HIGHLIGHTS

Beaver Creek has its origin in Beaver Basin, a wooded, rock-walled alpine valley that nestles at the base of several lofty peaks in the La Sal Mountains. Old mines scar the valley walls, but the creek that plunges steeply out of the valley is wild and unspoiled. After tumbling for several miles down a rocky, densely-timbered gorge, the creek crosses more miles of gentler, but still wooded mountainous terrain. At one point, the Castleton-Gateway road crosses the stream, providing convenient access not far above the beginning of its riotous journey down into Beaver Creek Canyon, a lovely, primitive, wooded gorge that winds between convoluted slickrock walls for 12 miles before joining the Dolores River gorge. Near the lower end of the stream's long, adventurous journey, most of its water is diverted into an irrigation ditch that serves to water ranchlands beside the Dolores. Just below the diversion, an old log corral marks the end of the short vehicle road that penetrates the lower end of Beaver Creek Canyon. The water diversion was first made by pioneer ranchers in the late 1800s. These minor man-made constructions at the lower end of the creek can hardly detract, however, from the remote, beautiful and un-spoiled hiking route that Beaver Creek provides in its long journey from alpine valley to desert gorge.

NOTES: The hike along the entire length of Beaver Creek is through very rugged and isolated mountain and canyon country, and should be attempted only by hikers who are well prepared and in top physical condition. The water in Beaver Creek, and its tributary streams and springs, can be considered potable with little or no treatment.

Cottonwood Canyon

TYPE OF TRAIL: canyon-stream.

TRAIL MILEAGE: about 7 miles, one way.

TIME TO HIKE: 1 to 2 days.

U.S.G.S. MAPS: Polar Mesa quadrangle.

HAZARDS: primitive, rugged and very remote canyon; free-climbing skills advisable.

SEASONS: early spring through late fall.

ACCESS: drive upriver from U.S. 163 on Utah 128 to Fisher Valley turn-off, about 5 miles beyond the paved turn-off into Castle Valley; drive graded dirt county road up Onion Creek to Fisher Valley; an off-road vehicle trail branches left about 1 mile after dirt road tops out of a steep grade onto flats of Fisher Valley; drive or hike this off-road trail ¼ mile to shallow upper wash of Cottonwood Canyon; this trail roughly parallels the developing canyon for 3 miles before climbing to canyon rim; for access or egress at lower end of Cottonwood Canyon, drive downriver from Gateway, Colorado, on west side of Dolores River; where graded dirt road ends, drive or hike off-road vehicle trail on downriver to its end at mouth of Cottonwood Canyon, about 13 road-miles from Gateway.

TRAIL SUMMARY: Hiking rugged and narrow Cottonwood Canyon from its origin in the Fisher Valley to its confluence with the Dolores River gorge provides an intimate look at one of the deepest, most remote and little-known redrock canyons in canyon country.

TRAIL HIGHLIGHTS

Cottonwood Canyon begins in the northeastern corner of Fisher Valley, an elevated, relatively flat area that is surrounded by lofty rock slopes on three sides. Part of Fisher Valley is drained by Onion

Creek as it flows through a gigantic gypsum outcropping and a narrow, winding canyon cut through dark-red Cutler sandstone, ultimately to cross Utah 128 and reach the Colorado River. Some of Onion Creek is also well worth hiking, where the county road bypasses its loops, and upstream from where the road starts up the steep grade into Fisher Valley. Exploring Onion Creek's tributary canyons can also be fascinating and rewarding. Cottonwood Canyon also drains part of Fisher Valley, but into the Dolores River gorge. The extreme upper end of Cottonwood Canyon, as it first cuts into the sediments of Fisher Valley, is a shallow drywash, but as the canyon plunges steeply downward, springs and such major tributaries as Hideout, Thompson and Burro canyons give Cottonwood enough water to form an intermittent, seasonal stream that is called Fisher Creek. Hiking down the upper half of Cottonwood Canyon is a rugged experience, as the canyon floor drops from 5600 to 4300 feet elevation in a little more than 7 miles, with most of that drop in the upper half. The rest of the canyon is more gently inclined, but only a little wider. The canyon twists and turns much as most canyon country gorges do, but it also stays quite narrow for its entire length. At its confluence with the Dolores River, Cottonwood Creek is over 900 feet below the rim of its sheer-walled canyon. The extremely deep, narrow nature of Cottonwood Canyon, the soaring rock pinnacles that stand at many canyon bends, plus the flowing stream and its attendant vegetation, trees and wildlife, all combine to make hiking this remote canyon an unforgettable experience.

NOTES: Hikers going down Cottonwood Canyon may find their progress expedited in a few places by free-climbing skills or ropes. In such places, going up is frequently easier and safer than going down. The road that goes down the west bank of the Dolores River from Gateway is very infrequently traveled. Hikers should not expect to hitchhike to Gateway from the mouth of Cottonwood Canyon, but walking this 13 miles of river gorge is a rewarding experience, whether on the road or beside the river.

Fisher Mesa Rim

TYPE OF TRAIL: canyon rim.

TRAIL MILEAGE: optional, up to 20 miles round trip.

TIME TO HIKE: optional, up to 4 days.

U.S.G.S. MAPS: Castle Valley and Polar Mesa quadrangles.

HAZARDS: no water; hazardous cliffs; rugged terrain.

SEASONS: early spring through late fall.

ACCESS: drive upriver from U.S. 163 on Utah 128 to Castle Valley turnoff; drive to end of paved road up Castle Valley; continue up graded dirt Forest Service road toward Gateway, Colorado; about 3 miles from end of pavement, turn left on an off-road vehicle trail that within ¼ mile angles steeply down onto Fisher Mesa near its northeastern rim; start rim hike here, or at several places farther along vehicle trail where it approaches the rim.

TRAIL SUMMARY: Rim-hiking spectacular Fisher Mesa provides continuous breathtaking views of the La Sal Mountains, Fisher Valley, a huge gypsum upthrust, the Onion Creek grottoes, the Fisher Towers, Richardson Amphitheater and the Colorado River, verdant Professor Valley, the upper Mary Jane Creek canyon-wilderness and many other outstanding canyon country features in the distance, plus an historic cabin and a wide variety of sandstone rim erosional forms.

TRAIL HIGHLIGHTS

Hiking the wooded Fisher Mesa rim in either direction affords an unbelievably spectacular bird's-eye view of a full-circle panorama of colorful, varied and unique canyon country geology. An off-road vehicle trail that is seldom traveled goes within about 1 mile of the high peninsula's slender tip, but rim-hikers will see this trail only in a few places where major drainages have cut into the mesa, forcing the trail toward its northeastern, higher rim. Hiking around the rim counter-clockwise, starting at the point where the vehicle trail first descends onto the mesa proper, hikers will first see the steep, verdant wall of Fisher Valley and its ranch and pastures, with still another lofty mesa rim beyond the valley. Farther along, the rim is directly above the gigantic "gypsqueeze" that separates Fisher Valley from labyrinthine Onion Creek and its tributaries where they have cut deeply into dark red Cutler sandstone. To the north of this unique geologic maze, the Fisher Towers stand in stately splendor, along the base of the same long, soaring cliff that walls Fisher Valley. Below these towers and the Onion Creek grottoes, the Colorado River winds for miles through a wide, high-walled canyon called Richardson Amphitheater. This stretch of the Colorado can be seen in its entirety from the tip of Fisher Mesa. About 4 miles along the northeastern rim of the mesa, hikers should watch for the collapsing remnants of an old cabin, built right on the rim out of rocks and logs. An old horseback trail descends from the cabin into Fisher Valley. The hike back along the southwestern rim of Fisher Mesa is considerably rougher and more circuitous, but it affords beautiful views down onto the ranches of lower Professor Valley and the eroded, colorful wilderness of upper Mary Jane Creek. Beyond Professor Valley to the west, giant Parriott Mesa, Castle Tower and other huge monoliths soar skyward, although still below the Fisher Mesa rim. A much shorter peninsula called Adobe Mesa, which is a smaller version of Fisher Mesa, juts toward the river from the La Sal Foothills. From almost anywhere along either rim of Fisher Mesa, the La Sal Mountains provide a breathtakingly beautiful alpine backdrop to the lower canyon scenery. Several major canyons slash deeply into the southwestern rim of Fisher Mesa, necessitating either long jaunts along their rims, or steep climbs down across the canyons. Either way, the going is not easy or fast. Hikers with limited time should either confine themselves to the northeastern rim and mesa tip, or carefully study the topographic map and terrain for the return hike along the southwestern rim. But whatever route is followed along the rimlands of this spectacular wilderness mesa, or how much of its total length is covered, hikers will find their time well spent because of the unparalleled scenic grandeur that surrounds Fisher Mesa on all sides.

NOTES: Although water may be found in occasional slickrock potholes or seeping springs on or near the Fisher Mesa rimlands, hikers should not rely upon this. The mesa rim can be more easily explored with one-day hikes by using an off-road vehicle along the mesa trail as a base. A large area of the mesa top near its end has been subjected to "chaining," a questionable but continuing range-management practice in which all the native trees are uprooted and killed by dragging a giant anchor chain between two large bulldozers. The rocky rim of the mesa has been largely undisturbed, but several hundred acres of the mesa interior now resemble a battlefield. Those who would like to rim-hike a mesa that has not been chained might try nearby Adobe Mesa. The off-road vehicle trail onto this mesa leaves the same Forest Service road 1¾ miles beyond the end of the paved Castle Valley road.

Fisher Towers

TYPE OF TRAIL: designated.

TRAIL MILEAGE: 4½ miles, round trip.

TIME TO HIKE: 3 to 6 hours.

U.S.G.S. MAPS: Castle Valley quadrangle.

HAZARDS: steep trail, no water.

SEASONS: any season, but may be difficult to reach some winters.

ACCESS: drive upriver from U.S. 163 on Utah 128 for about 20 miles; turn right onto graded dirt road marked by small sign; go 2 miles to parking-picnic area at base of towers; trail starts here.

TRAIL SUMMARY: The Fisher Towers trail takes hikers along a winding, picturesque route through a series of gigantic redrock spires and up onto a high ridge which affords a sweeping, panoramic view of a beautiful stretch of the Colorado River gorge in one direction, and an immense upthrust of gypsum in the other.

TRAIL HIGHLIGHTS

The Fisher Towers stand silent guard over the mouth of unique Fisher Valley within sight of the Colorado River. The hiking trail immediately enters a lofty maze of tall, slender spires that eons of erosion have carved from ancient Moenkopi and Cutler sandstone. The towers and surrounding terrain are dark red in color. Most of the towers have vertical fluting cut by rain and, oddly, are coated with what appears to be soft, dry mud. The tops of many towers are eroded into weird shapes that defy description. The trail winds through the soaring sandstone spires, often clinging to steep slopes above sharply cut arroyos filled with the gargoyle shapes of weathered sandstone. As the trail ascends, it passes dozens of slender, skyscraping monoliths, offers sweeping views of the green-bordered, meandering Colorado River in sheer-walled Richardson Amphitheater, plus occasional glimpses of Castle Tower and the Priest and Nuns spires in the distance. As the trail tops out of its climb, it goes near the base of the Titan, the tallest of the Fisher Towers. The Titan soars over 900 feet above its base, and has been scaled at least twice, once by a National Geographic team. Beyond the Titan, the trail follows the summit of a ridge for about ½ mile before ending. The view from this ridge is magnificent in all directions. To the east, an immense gypsum upthrust sprawls across Fisher Valley. Beyond this mass of light-colored minerals set in dark red sandstone, the meadows of upper Fisher Valley lie below high sandstone cliffs. These in turn are dominated by the still higher La Sal Mountains. Below the "gypsqueeze," the redrock grottoes of Onion Creek are visible, and toward the west and north the broad river gorge of the Colorado lies below mighty talus slopes that are topped by sheer-walled sandstone cliffs hundreds of feet high. This entire setting is exceptionally colorful in the winter, with a light patina of snow lending contrast to the dark red rock.

NOTES: The Fisher Towers trail is shown on a Bureau of Land Management brochure available at the Federal Building, 446 South Main Street, Moab. These brochures are sometimes available at the head of the hiking trail. An article describing one Fisher Towers climb appeared in the November 1962 issue of *National Geographic* magazine.

La Sal Mountains

TYPE OF TRAILS: mountain.

TRAIL MILEAGE: optional, unlimited.

TIME TO HIKE: optional, unlimited.

U.S.G.S. MAPS: Castle Valley, Polar Mesa, La Sal and La Sal Junction quadrangles.

SEASONS: best from late spring through fall, but may be traveled using snowshoes or cross-country skis when snow precludes normal hiking.

HAZARDS: very steep slopes; deep canyons; dangerous slopes of loose rubble; dense vegetation in places.

ACCESS: western slopes are accessible via La Sal Mountain Loop Road and side roads to Warner Lake, Oowah Lake and up to Geyser Pass; off-road vehicle trail from Pack Creek picnic grounds to La Sal Pass provides further access from the west; Utah 46 and various county and Forest Service roads provide access from the south and southeast; road to Buckeye Reservoir from Paradox Valley in Colorado, plus connecting Forest Service roads, provide access from the east; access from the north is via the Castleton-Gateway Forest Service and county road and connecting Forest Service roads; between these access routes, a network of Forest Service roads and off-road vehicle trails provide access to La Sal Mountains backcountry; some of these roads and trails are shown on U.S.G.S. topographic maps of the area and on the large Forest Service map described in the area introduction; there is no comprehensive map of the vehicle roads and trails, and hiking trails and routes, in the La Sal Mountains.

TRAIL SUMMARY: Although there are a few interconnecting, poorly maintained and unmarked primitive hiking trails within the La Sal Mountains, most of the hiking there is a combination of following seldom used or abandoned off-road vehicle trails plus self-guiding through rugged mountain wilderness, with all the usual forests, wildlife, streams, alpine meadows, old log cabins, abandoned mines and similar highlights to be found in all western mountains of similar elevation.

TRAIL HIGHLIGHTS

The following list of "primitive" hiking trails was taken from an unpublished Forest Service report. Hikers will need to refer to U.S.G.S. and Forest Service maps for approximate routes of the trails, and for locations of the geographic features and roads and off-road vehicle trails that provide trail access and egress. Hikers are warned that these "primitive" hiking trails are poorly marked, if at all, not maintained and often difficult to find and follow. The mileages given are from the Forest Service report. They should be considered minimums.

Miners Basin - Warner Lake (1½ miles): The trail begins in Miners Basin, climbs over a steep ridge to the wooded meadows of Warner Lake.

Warner Lake-Oowah Lake (1½ miles): The trail begins by crossing the low dam, continues through dense woods to turn right onto a vehicle trail for a short distance, left onto an abandoned vehicle trail, then right along a well-defined path down into the Mill Creek drainage to the Lake Oowah road and up that road to the lake.

Lake Oowah - Boren Mesa (2½ miles): The trail starts by crossing the Lake Oowah dam, continues up a steep grade then levels off across Boren Mesa. Trail then drops down a steep grade into Horse Creek Canyon and out again to continue around the mountain contours to the Geyser Pass Road in the lower Gold Basin area.

Brumley (3½ miles): This trail continues the Boren Mesa trail from the Geyser Pass Road, again following the mountain contours through Brumley and Dorry canyons to the La Sal Pass off-road vehicle trail.

Hells Canyon - Pack Creek (3 miles): This trail continues the Brumley trail from the La Sal Pass vehicle trail, drops steeply into Hells Canyon and out, follows a rocky ridge then drops steeply into the Pack Creek drainage and down past an old cabin and on to the Pack Creek picnic area and road via an old off-road vehicle trail.

The above trail segments form a continuous route from a fairly easy access point in Miners Basin to the gravelled road that goes to the Pack Creek picnic area. Along this route, spur trails are listed in the Forest Service report as follows:

Miners Basin - Bachelor Basin (1½ miles): Trail begins at Miners Basin, crosses an open meadow into aspen trees, climbs a steep, rocky grade, drops sharply into Bachelor Basin to follow an off-road vehicle trail on out to a Forest Service road.

Bachelor Basin - Castle Creek (4 miles): This spur trail forks from the Bachelor Basin trail at an ill-defined point after following the vehicle trail down for about 2 miles, then continues through dense brush to the Castle Creek bridge, where the Castleton-Gateway road pavement ends.

Burro Pass (4 miles): Trail spurs from the Warner - Oowah trail by leaving the vehicle trail before reaching Oowah Lake, then continuing up the Mill Creek drainage to the junction of the Wet and Dry Forks of the creek, where the trail splits. Trail to the left up Dry Fork goes up the drainage to near its end, climbs over a ridge then drops into Beaver Basin drainage. Trail to the right up Wet Fork continues up toward Burro Pass, then down to the Geyser Pass road.

Lake Oowah - Clark Lake (2½ miles): Trail begins at Lake Oowah, continues uphill behind the Oowah campground along a ridge, drops to Clark Lake then continues to the Geyser Pass Road.

La Sal Pass - Pole Canyon (6½ miles): Trail begins at La Sal Pass along the vehicle trail toward the west, follows the Pack Creek drainage above the Hells Canyon - Pack Creek trail, reaches that trail, proceeds to a ridge top, up a steep slope, drops steeply into the head of Lackey Basin, climbs out again to continue along a ridge to a fork. Right fork goes down Doe Canyon to the Doe Canyon Forest Service road. Left fork goes down Pole Canyon to the La Sal Pass Forest Service road.

The foregoing unofficial Forest Service trail routes will give hikers a sample of La Sal Mountain country and will undoubtedly suggest other even more primitive routes to explore. Hikers who do not mind following abandoned or seldom-used off-road vehicle trails will find a whole interconnecting network of these in the La Sals, most of them made by miners or ranchers in earlier days. One example of such a vehicle trail and its spurs worth hiking is the one from the Pack Creek picnic area to La Sal Pass and on east to Forest Service road #129. There are many others.

NOTES: The La Sal Mountains are geologically young and hence very steep, with sharply eroded slopes, drainage lines and canyons. Hikers who intend to wilderness hike in these mountains should be well-equipped, experienced and in top physical condition. Potable water is plentiful in the La Sals, making lengthy backpacking feasible.

Mill Creek Canyon

TYPE OF TRAIL: canyon-stream.

TRAIL MILEAGE: optional, up to 15 miles along main canyon, plus 18 additional miles of major tributary canyons.

TIME TO HIKE: optional, up to several days.

U.S.G.S. MAPS: Moab, Castle Valley and La Sal Junction quadrangles.

HAZARDS: very rugged route in places; hazardous drops.

SEASONS: spring through fall; lower stretches can be hiked in winter when snow is light.

ACCESS: for access to lower end of canyon, drive south on 4th East in Moab; turn east on Mill Creek Road; turn left on road near drive-in theater; drive this dirt road to its end at an old dam on Mill Creek; hikeable canyon begins here; for access or egress at upper end of main canyon, drive La Sal Mountain Loop Road; enter or leave Mill Creek Canyon where road to Oowah Lake leaves Loop Road; for access or egress to main canyon about 8 miles above the old dam, drive old highway from Moab up Spanish Valley; turn left onto Flat Pass off-road vehicle trail about 8 miles from Moab; trail reaches Mill Creek after about 4 miles; for another access into North Fork of Mill Creek, turn off of Mill Creek Road in Moab onto Sand Flats Road, just before Mill Creek bridge; stay on rough, graded dirt Sand Flats Road into Rill Creek Canyon, just beyond a spring-fed water tank and about 9 miles from Mill Creek Road; hike down into Rill Creek Canyon, which joins the North Fork of Mill Creek Canyon.

TRAIL SUMMARY: Hiking Mill Creek Canyon and its major tributary canyons can provide several days of canyon-stream beauty, with high canyon walls, springs, pools, beaver dams, falls, arches, archeological sites and completely unspoiled wilderness in the tributary canyons.

TRAIL HIGHLIGHTS

The main canyon of Mill Creek begins high in the La Sals, where the Loop Road crosses Mill Creek, and continues downward through wild and rugged slickrock country to open into Moab Valley just east of Moab. About ½ mile above the old dam near the lower end of the canyon, the North Fork of Mill Creek cuts into still more slickrock wilderness, with two major and several minor branches. Of these, Rill Creek Canyon and Burkholder Draw are well worth hiking. The main canyon above the old dam winds and twists between picturesque slickrock walls for most of its length, passing one bottomland development about 3 miles above the dam, and an old ranch near where the Flat Pass vehicle trail crosses the creek. Another vehicle trail parallels the creek for a short distance above the first development, then climbs onto higher ground. Mill Creek is a tumbling, brawling perennial creek for its entire length, affording ample opportunity for cooling off during the warmer months. The North Fork also has a flowing, perennial stream, fed in part by its major tributaries, Rill and Burkholder. About 2½ miles up North Fork, a short spur canyon shelters Otho Natural Bridge. The North Fork proper ends, so far as hiking is concerned, at the base of Wilson and South Mesas, but Rill and Burkholder both offer more unusual opportunities for exploring this fascinating and lovely canyon system. Rill is an intermittent, seasonal stream, but has countless seeping springs, slickrock pools, lush vegetation and, near its upper end, gigantic caves and dry waterfalls. It is possible to hike up out of Rill Creek Canyon to the Sand Flats Road almost anywhere along its upper 2 miles. Burkholder Draw branches from Rill Creek Canyon about 2 miles above its North Fork confluence. After about 3 miles of beautiful wilderness canyon similar to Rill, the drainage climbs very steeply into a wooded, rock-walled basin known as Valley of the Gnomes. There are three arches of various sizes in these walls, and in the vicinity of a great slickrock mass on the left, odd-shaped rock columns topped with white caprocks resembling monstrous "gnomes." One such that is exceptionally tall is known as "King of the Gnomes." Just beyond this unusual little valley, the drainage line reaches the Sand Flats Road.

NOTES: For the most part, the water in the entire Mill Creek Canyon system may be considered potable, although the stream in the main canyon may be somewhat polluted by grazing cattle. With care, it is possible to drive a low-geared highway vehicle with good clearances up the Sand Flats Road as far as the head of Burkholder Draw, but an off-road vehicle is preferable. Those hiking this canyon-stream system should be prepared for wading in many places, and for rather strenuous climbing in the upper ends of each canyon branch.

Negro Bill Canyon

TYPE OF TRAIL: canyon-stream.

TRAIL MILEAGE: optional, up to 10 miles or more.

TIME TO HIKE: optional, up to 2 days or more.

U.S.G.S. MAPS: Moab and Castle Valley quadrangles.

HAZARDS: upper end steep with hazardous drops; poison oak in a few places.

SEASONS: early spring through late fall; can be hiked winter when snow is light.

ACCESS: drive upriver from U.S. 163 on Utah 128 for 3 miles to lower end of Negro Bill Canyon; access or egress at upper end of canyon is via off-road vehicle trail spur to the left from Sand Flats Road at spring-fed water tank.

TRAIL SUMMARY: The Negro Bill Canyon system cuts deeply into the elevated slickrock wilderness region between Moab Valley and Castle Valley, with all of the main canyon and several of the branches well worth exploring.

TRAIL HIGHLIGHTS

For the first 6 miles or so above its junction with the Colorado River gorge, Negro Bill Canyon has a perennial stream fed by numerous springs, with occasional seeps in its upper stretches and major branches. The canyon cuts through Navajo sandstone slickrock for most of its length, thus creating high, spectacular cliffs, giant alcoves, age-patinaed walls, terraced shelves and great domes and fins, all looming above a lovely, winding stream that shelters a variety of aquatic life and is bordered by lush, water-loving plants and trees. The first half mile of the canyon is made somewhat unsightly by the remnants of earlier use and local abuse, but the rest of the canyon system is unspoiled, lovely desert-canyon wilderness at its best. The second side-canyon on the right, about 1½ miles from the highway, is only ½ mile long and has huge Morning Glory Natural Bridge at its upper end. This awe-inspiring bridge is the fifth widest natural span in the country. Most of the other side-canyons are relatively dry, but well worth exploring for hikers interested in penetrating some wild canyon to the highway, or climb out its upper end to the Sand Flats Road. The climb will be strenuous and hazardous, and should be attempted only by those with free-climbing skills and in good physical condition.

NOTES: Hikers attempting to go down Negro Bill Canyon from its upper end will find climbing rope and rappelling skills very useful. It is possible to leave this canyon system via most of its eastern tributaries, then return to the Sand Flats Road via the rarely used off-road vehicle trails that lie to the west of Porcupine Rim. A hike up to Morning Glory Natural Bridge, and perhaps a little farther up the main canyon, then back to the highway, provides an excellent one-day look at the beauty and variety in Negro Bill Canyon.

Porcupine Rim

TYPE OF TRAIL: canyon rim.

TRAIL MILEAGE: optional, up to 20 miles round trip or more.

TIME TO HIKE: optional, up to several days.

U.S.G.S. MAPS: Castle Valley quadrangle.

HAZARDS: no water; hazardous cliffs.

SEASONS: spring through late fall; not accessible in the winter or early spring.

ACCESS: turn onto Mill Creek Road from 4th East in Moab; turn onto Sand Flats Road; drive up this rough, steep, graded dirt road for about 12 miles; a couple of hundred yards beyond the National Forest boundary, drive or hike left along off-road vehicle trail here for about ½ mile to Porcupine Rim.

TRAIL SUMMARY: Hiking all or any portion of Porcupine Rim, the high and isolated southwestern rim of spectacularly beautiful Castle Valley, provides endless breathtaking views across that valley, of major geologic features beyond, of the Colorado River gorge in the Richardson Amphitheater area, the lofty La Sal Mountains and the redrock wilderness of Negro Bill Canyon and its many tributaries, as well as a close look at a wide variety of sandstone erosional forms and high-desert plant life.

TRAIL HIGHLIGHTS

The easiest way to reach Porcupine Rim is from the Sand Flats Road, just within the National Forest boundary. The short vehicle trail to the rim here was constructed in support of running a set of power lines down from the rim into upper Castle Valley. Other than a few places where a rarely-used off-road vehicle trail approaches the rim, these power lines are the only human traces along the entire spectacular length of Porcupine Rim. The rim extends toward the La Sals from the power line site, and that stretch is well worth hiking for a short distance, but most of the rim is in the other direction. A small, isolated homestead called Porcupine Ranch is directly below the rim here. Unfortunately, the upper part of Castle Valley, from Round Mountain, a small igneous peak near the center of Castle Valley, on up to the National Forest boundary has been transferred from the Bureau of Land Management to State ownership, so more developments in this relatively unspoiled part of the beautiful valley can be expected. Below the rim, on down toward the river, the cultivated fields and checkerboard roads of a rural subdivision mar the natural beauty of the valley, but the great red towers and mesas on the far side of the valley and beyond enhance the broad panoramic view. Since the upper stretches of Porcupine Rim are higher than the surrounding nearby canyon country, rim hikers are afforded outstanding full-circle views. As the rim reaches the Colorado River gorge high above White Ranch, it continues along the rim of that gorge around a great river loop. The high peninsula formed by that loop is called Mat Martin Point. Hikers prepared for a still longer jaunt through this rarely seen canyon wilderness might consider continuing around Mat Martin Point, staying near the river gorge rim to Drinks Canyon, cutting across Jackass Canyon to Coffee Pot Rock, following contours southeastward, dropping down into one of the northeastern tributary canyons of Negro Bill Canyon then going down Negro Bill Canyon to Utah 128. This entire route might take as long as 5 days and cover 30 rugged but beautiful miles.

NOTES: While hiking Porcupine Rim is one highlight in the sandstone wilderness between Castle Valley and Moab Valley, the rim should also be considered an access route to the more remote parts of this isolated area. While the rim, itself, may lack water other than in an occasional pothole, there are springs in the general area between the rim and the various Negro Bill Canyon tributaries that could support backpack campers.

Professor Valley

TYPE OF TRAIL: canyon-stream.

TRAIL MILEAGE: optional, up to 10 miles round trip.

TIME TO HIKE: optional, up to 1 day.

U.S.G.S. MAPS: Castle Valley quadrangle.

HAZARDS: none.

SEASONS: early spring through late fall; can be hiked winter when snow is light.

ACCESS: drive upriver from U.S. 163 on Utah 128 to about 3 miles beyond Castle Valley turn-off; turn right onto graded road; go to end of road, where Mary Jane Creek is diverted into an irrigation ditch; hike up the flowing stream canyon.

TRAIL SUMMARY: Mary Jane Creek flows through an area of very colorful, eroded sandstone formations, affording hikers an easy route into unspoiled upper Professor Valley and a close look at towering Adobe and Fisher Mesas that wall this beautiful and unusual wilderness valley.

TRAIL HIGHLIGHTS

Mary Jane Creek begins as a multiple-source series of trickling streams and springs high on the slopes of adjacent Fisher and Adobe Mesas. As the water gathers at the bases of these gigantic cliffs, it flows a winding course through softer valley deposits of the Cutler Formation, to be joined just above the ranches in the lower valley by intermittent, seasonal Professor Creek, which gives its name to the combined watershed on to the Colorado River. Mary Jane Creek, above where it is diverted for irrigation, is bordered by water-loving vegetation and serves as a focal point for the diverse wildlife in the upper, primitive part of the valley. Hiking the creek affords endless examples of unusual and lovely sandstone erosional forms, and springtime hikers will find quite a selection of annual and perennial wildflowers. Autumn brings blossoms to still other species. Hikers will also find it interesting to go up the dryer Professor Creek tributary to its origin near the base of soaring Castle Tower. This area, too, exhibits an assortment of colorful sandstone erosional forms.

NOTES: The waters of Mary Jane Creek are highly mineralized, but may be considered potable by those not sensitive to such mineralization. The cottonwood and tamarisk of lower Professor Valley provide vivid displays of color in late autumn.

Sand Flats

TYPE OF TRAIL: slickrock.

TRAIL MILEAGE: optional.

TIME TO HIKE: optional.

U.S.G.S. MAPS: Moab and Castle Valley quadrangles.

HAZARDS: no water; hazardous drops.

SEASONS: best during cooler months of spring or fall, but may be hiked in the summer; snow on slickrock precludes hiking.

ACCESS: turn onto Mill Creek Road from 4th East in Moab; turn left onto Sand Flats Road; continue for about 3 miles on this rough, steep, graded-dirt road to just beyond trailhead for the BLM Slickrock Bike Trail; drive toward slickrock masses to southwest of road along branching off-road vehicle trails for next 4 miles, or hike across to slickrock from anywhere along this stretch of road.

TRAIL SUMMARY: Exploring the great slickrock masses that border the lower end of the Mill Creek Canyon system provides hikers a close look at one of the most novel and beautiful erosional forms in canyon country, as well as enchanting views down into remote stretches of the two major forks of Mill Creek.

TRAIL HIGHLIGHTS

Exploring the 4 mile long expanse of eroded Navajo sandstone that lies above and to the north of the Mill Creek canyon system is more like finding the way through a maze than hiking a conventional trail route. Discovering a way through such extensive masses of "petrified sand dunes" is a challenge. Even though the hiker has many optional routes, around and between slickrock domes, ridges and fins, or up onto and along those weathered rock masses, getting from one point to another is difficult. Steep drops, unjumpable gaps, narrow chasms choked with brush and sheer rock walls are common hazards to straightforward progress in such a sandstone slickrock labyrinth. Even so, slickrock hiking offers rewards to be found nowhere else in the nation, and this particular area of slickrock provides a convenient place to sample such hiking, an area that is quite primitive and unspoiled, despite its close proximity to a small city.

NOTES: There are other Navajo sandstone slickrock masses within easy walking distance of the Sand Flats Road almost everywhere until it climbs up onto Wilson Mesa. One exceptionally good area is in the vicinity of upper Burkholder Draw, Section 3, T 26 S, R 23 E of the Castle Valley quadrangle map.

Hermit

For hours my wife and I had slowly worked our way along the Fisher Mesa rim, sometimes following a long-abandoned, overgrown vehicle trail just back from the rim, but mostly hiking directly on the tree-studded slickrock rim.

We were searching for an ancient hermit's cabin that had been reported to us by a canyon country old-timer. All we had to guide us were some vague verbal descriptions and a crude pencil sketch, with only the general relationship of major features shown on that map—no mileages. Although we had fallen victim to the vagueness of old memories before, we were determined to find this cabin.

Our search of the broken, wooden rimlands continued. Was the cabin on the rocky rim itself, or in some thick grove of trees just back from the rim? Our source had been vague about that, too. Strange, how some articulate old-timers can draw complete word-pictures of places they have been decades before, while others, try as they may, have great difficulty in translating even their dearest memories into words.

Baffled, hours after our search had started, we were about to give up and head home. The day was late, and we were not prepared to camp out. I was disgusted and ready to go, but my patient wife urged, "Just one more stretch of rim."

And her intuition paid off. There, right on the rim, was what had to be the cabin, although it was in an advanced stage of collapse and barely recognizable as a human structure from even a short distance away.

It was built partly under a great, overhanging slab of rock, with low rock walls and crude timbers used to extend the shallow cavern. Other un-milled timbers had been used to roof over the cave annex, and a "store-bought" door that now hung crazily from one hinge had provided weather-proof access. A crude stone fireplace-kitchen occupied one corner.

We searched around and found the eroded traces of a pack animal trail that connected the high rim with Fisher Valley far below. No doubt, this was the only practical access to the rim when the cabin was built, making its builder and occupant a hermit in fact, if not intent.

After another half hour of musing over this isolated, almost forgotten vignette of canyon country history, we headed home, more than a little glad to have been born a century later.

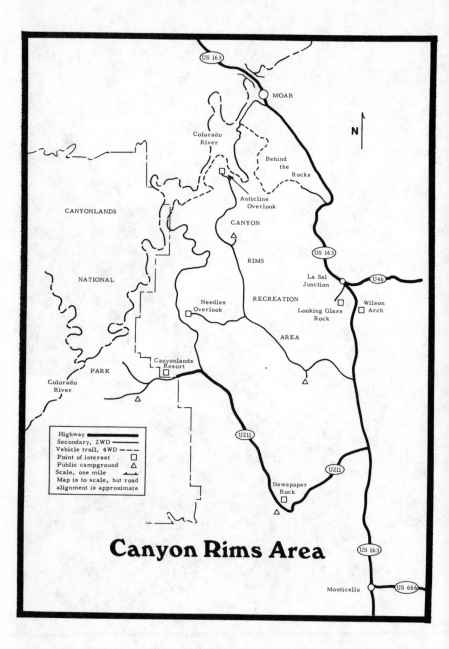

Canyon Rims Area

US 163

MOAB

N

Colorado
River

Behind
the
Rocks

Anticline
Overlook

CANYONLANDS

CANYON

RIMS

US 163

La Sal
Junction

U 46

NATIONAL

RECREATION

Needles
Overlook

Looking Glass
Rock

Wilson
Arch

AREA

Canyonlands
Resort

PARK

Colorado
River

U 211

U 211

Newspaper
Rock

US 163

Highway
Secondary, 2WD
Vehicle trail, 4WD
Point of interest ☐
Public campground △
Scale, one mile
Map is to scale, but road
alignment is approximate

Monticello

US 666

94

Canyon Rims Area

AREA NAME: this area was named after Canyon Rims Recreation Area, an immense, sprawling plateau region that dominates the center of this area.

AREA BOUNDARIES: U.S. 163, Colorado River, Utah 211 and its extension in Canyonlands National Park.

U.S.G.S. TOPOGRAPHIC MAPS THAT COVER THE AREA: Moab, LaSal Junction, Hatch Point, Hatch Rock, Harts Point and The Needles quadrangles.

GENERAL TOPOGRAPHY: northeastern part is elevated, highly eroded masses of sandstone slickrock bordered on three sides by deep, spectacular canyons, fading into sand flats toward the south and cut by numerous lesser canyon systems; eastern part along U.S. 163 is open, rolling desert plains studded with gigantic rock outcroppings and cut by deep canyon systems toward the west to form a long, winding rim high above the eastern part of Canyonlands National Park; area between the rim and park is a maze of red-rock lowlands and still more canyons that cut downward toward the Colorado River gorge.

SUGGESTED BASE CAMPS: motels or commercial campgrounds in Moab and at Canyonlands Resort; developed public campgrounds in Canyon Rims Recreation Area, at Newspaper Rock State Historical Monument and in the Needles District of Canyonlands National Park; primitive camping is permitted almost anywhere within the area except in Canyonlands National Park; contact park rangers for current regulations there.

ACCESS ROUTES:. U.S. 163, Cane Creek Road, Utah 211 and its park extension, county and BLM roads and off-road vehicle trails as shown on the area map.

AREA NOTES:
1. Despite its title and huge size, Canyon Rims Recreation Area contains no designated trails other than walks around its two developed overlooks and a short "nature trail" out of Windwhistle Campground. There is, however, endless primitive hiking in the recreation area's desert washes and slickrock masses, along its many miles of canyon rims, and up the great canyon systems below those rims. Hikers who

wish to explore the recreation area can use the area map for access and appropriate topographic maps for detailed guidance.

2. The lowlands between the cliffs of Canyon Rims Recreation Area and the Colorado River gorge are the largest single exposure of dark red Cutler deposits in canyon country. This weirdly-eroded landscape of almost unrelieved red rock more closely resembles a scene on Mars than anywhere on Earth.

3. Pronghorn antelope have been "planted" in the Canyon Rims Recreation Area and are quite often seen individually or in small herds.

Tracks

My wife and I were hiking up a steep, narrow draw with a professional rockhound friend. The route climbed steeply toward an echoing slickrock grotto through great slabs of Kayenta sandstone that were covered with the ornate bas-relief of mud-casts.

Above and beyond this tricky dry waterfall, we visited and photographed a lovely arch, enjoyed the panoramic view then headed back down. As we went, we somehow got onto the subject of petrified dinosaur tracks. There were a few of these in the vicinity, in the same rock formation through which we were descending.

Our friend slowed and started looking closely at some separating rock layers, then pointed excitedly at a two-foot slab covered with strange indentations and ridges. We all three examined the greenish-tinged sandstone slab for several minutes, conjecturing about what beastie might have made such tracks in the mud of this erstwhile lakeshore or shallow stream.

Our rockhound friend sagely concluded that the "tracks" just had to be those of a crawling turtle. As he and my wife continued to discuss the "turtle tracks," I wandered off down the slope, looking carefully at the ground as I went, watching for more unusual rock surfaces. Within a few yards I crossed a tiny drywash. The bottom of the wash was solid rock.

And there, plain as day in that 30-foot exposure of Kayenta sandstone, were dozens of large, three-toed tracks, deeply impressed in the solid wash bottom. Dinosaur tracks, beyond a doubt! We had walked right across them on our way up without seeing them! But coming back, my head was thinking "tracks," and my eyes were seeking track patterns — and found them, to the utter chagrin of our rockhounding friend.

My discovery site was later declared by a knowledgeable scientist to be "probably one of the best in Utah." A nice find, indeed, in a state renowned for its paleontological wonders.

Sadly, our friend's "turtle tracks" slab turned out to be nothing more than a peculiar chunk of ripplerock, something very common in canyon country.

Amasa Back

TYPE OF TRAIL: canyon rim.

TRAIL MILEAGE: optional.

TIME TO HIKE: optional, up to 3 days or more.

U.S.G.S. MAPS: Moab and Hatch Point quadrangles.

HAZARDS: no water; hazardous cliffs; isolated area.

SEASONS: best during cooler months of spring and fall, but may be hiked in summer or winter when snow is light.

ACCESS: drive down river from U.S. 163 on Cane Creek Road in Moab; after pavement ends, drive up Cane Creek Canyon on gravel road for about 1¼ miles; drive or hike down off-road vehicle trail into canyon bottom, then continue on same trail up onto benchlands on other side of gorge; for the first mile or more, vehicle trail follows only practical route up onto highlands of Amasa Back.

TRAIL SUMMARY: Hiking up onto Amasa Back via the rarely used off-road vehicle trail and beyond provides a good look at an elevated slickrock mesa that is surrounded on all sides by deep, picturesque canyons.

TRAIL HIGHLIGHTS

A highly eroded, rarely used off-road vehicle trail provides practical access up onto a slickrock wilderness plateau that is rarely visited by anyone. The plateau, called Amasa Back, is surrounded on three sides by the Colorado River gorge and on the fourth side by deeply incised Cane Creek Canyon. The highest point on the plateau is almost 1000 feet above the river, and canyon rims around the plateau approach this height in several places, offering spectacular views beyond the river gorge of such major features as Behind-the-Rocks, the La Sal Mountains, Poison Spider Mesa, Dead Horse Point, Island in the Sky and the gigantic abandoned meander, or "rincon," of the Colorado called Jackson Hole. Hikers may choose to rim-hike Amasa Back wherever possible, and also explore the wilderness interior of the 6-mile long mesa. The vehicle trail that provides access up onto the plateau can be followed to several interesting highlights in its southern part. At the first trail fork, the left fork goes into a picturesque box-end canyon that usually has some water in a pool at its upper end. The right fork climbs higher, then forks again. This right fork crosses the mesa through a dunes area to reach the river gorge rim where a pipeline drops downward. The rim viewpoint overlooks the first 5 miles of the Colorado River gorge below Moab Valley, and the southern part of Poison Spider Mesa. The left fork of the vehicle trail goes on across the slender "neck" of Amasa Back, to where the pipeline and several utility lines cross the mesa. Beyond this point, the great northern projection of Amasa Back invites hikers to explore the rim, and the huge Navajo sandstone slickrock area at its far end. It is also possible to hike along rock terraces at various levels, and even down to the river, except for a stretch where sheer rock walls in the vicinity of "The Billboard" leave no terraces.

NOTES: Any water on this mesa should be potable for backpack camping use with only minor purification. Access to Amasa Back can also be had by crossing the Colorado in a boat from many places along Utah 279, beginning about 4 miles downriver from Moab Valley. Funnel Arch is visible from many places along the first mile or 2 of the vehicle trail and its left fork. The arch stands high on an isolated terrace on the other side of lower Cane Creek Canyon. It is also possible for hikers with climbing skills to get onto Amasa Back from the summit ridge north of Hurrah Pass.

Behind-the-Rocks

TYPE OF TRAIL: slickrock.

TRAIL MILEAGE: optional.

TIME TO HIKE: optional.

U.S.G.S. MAPS: Moab, La Sal Junction and Hatch Point quadrangles.

HAZARDS: no reliable water; hazardous cliffs and drops; isolated area.

SEASONS: best during cooler months of spring or fall, but may be hiked in summer or winter when snow is light.

ACCESS: for access at south end, drive south on U.S. 163 for 13 miles from center of Moab; turn right on rough graded dirt road; drive or hike this road and several branching off-road vehicle trails into sand-and-slickrock maze to the north; to enter area's northern end, drive down river from Moab on Cane Creek Road; about 1 mile below the river portal, drive or hike off-road vehicle trail up into Behind-the-Rocks; to enter from northwest, drive Cane Creek Road downriver to end of pavement; drive or hike off-road vehicle trail up Pritchett Canyon into Behind-the-Rocks.

TRAIL SUMMARY: Weeks could be spent exploring the 50 square mile labyrinth of slickrock fins and domes, arches, giant caverns, sand dunes, deeply cut canyons and lofty rimlands of Behind-the-Rocks.

TRAIL HIGHLIGHTS

Behind-the-Rocks is a vast, elevated region that lies between Moab Valley and Cane Creek Canyon. It is defined on the north by the meandering gorge of the Colorado River, and on the south by the broad sand flats just north of Bridger Jack Mesa. Within this 50 square miles of primitive canyon country is a region of spectacular scenery, great mazes of giant sandstone fins, many arches, natural bridges and windows, deep canyon systems, tall spires, large spring-fed pools, archeological sites, wildlife and wildly distorted and eroded rock strata. Although three main off-road vehicle trails penetrate this ruggedly beautiful area, most of it can be explored only on foot, with the vehicle trails used for convenient access. Hikers can use any of the access routes noted, then continue exploring beyond the trails to suit their interests. The southern access route enters more open country, where there are several interesting arches along the rim of Spanish Valley and in a large slickrock mass about 5 miles from the highway. The northern access route climbs steeply to the high rim above the town of Moab, then penetrates an area containing several scattered archeological sites, a drainage line that ends at a large pool of water on the rim of the Colorado River gorge and other highlights. This route provides the quickest access into an immense area of slickrock fins. The Pritchett Canyon access route follows a slickrock gorge for miles, providing many opportunities for hikers to climb out into adjacent slickrock highland areas. Access to Halls Bridge, Pritchett Arch and several unnamed spans is via this route. Experienced, well-prepared hikers might want to enter at either end of this 10 mile long sandstone labyrinth, explore for several days, seeking out the scattered sources of water along the way, then leave via the opposite end. It is quite probable that much of Behind-the-Rocks has never been seen except from the air, which leaves ample room for new discoveries of such things as archeological sites and natural spans.

NOTES: Hikers who plan more than 1-day hikes into Behind-the-Rocks from established vehicle trails should be prepared for rugged and difficult terrains, and be experienced at locating the scattered sources of water that exist on such eroded desert mesas. Since domestic grazing is generally limited to the southernmost part of this area, any water found should be potable with only minor purification. Upper Hunter Wash has several branching canyons worth exploring. Hikers who enjoy canyon rim hiking will find that the vehicle trail that goes through Behind-the-Rocks on the west side offers convenient access to the high rim of Cane Creek Canyon in several places.

Cane Creek Canyon

TYPE OF TRAIL: canyon-stream.

TRAIL MILEAGE: optional, up to 19 miles or more.

TIME TO HIKE: optional, up to 3 days or more.

U.S.G.S. MAPS: Moab, Hatch Point and La Sal Junction quadrangles.

HAZARDS: hazardous drops, upper end; isolated area.

SEASONS: best during cooler months of spring or fall, but may be hiked in summer or winter when snow is light.

ACCESS: for access at upper end, drive south from Moab on U.S. 163 for about 16 miles to "Hole in the Rock" home-in-a-cave; hike down into wash bottom to west of highway; this is beginning of canyon that offers the most attractive hiking; for access or egress at lower end of Cane Creek Canyon, drive downriver from Moab on Cane Creek Road; this road becomes gravelled near mouth of Cane Creek Canyon, enters canyon, climbs high above the lower gorge for several miles before dropping down into it, then penetrates the first 3 miles of the broad central canyon, thus providing hikers access at many points.

TRAIL SUMMARY: Hiking the length of this well-watered, 19-mile long canyon system will afford an excellent and varied look at an exceptionally magnificent redrock canyon system that is very narrow and deep at each end, with broad and spectacular stretches in the middle.

TRAIL HIGHLIGHTS

An old off-road vehicle trail travels the length of this great, branching canyon system, but this trail is generally impassable due to washouts, leaving the upper 11 miles of the canyon to hikers. Although a gravelled county road penetrates the lower 8 miles of this long gorge, the last 2½ miles of this stretch provides excellent hiking along the winding canyon bottom, far below the road. There is always enough water along the water course in the canyon to supply hikers who wish to spend several days exploring the canyon and its major tributaries. Cane Creek, as it leaves U.S. 163, first goes down a fairly level, wooded canyon. At about 1½ miles from the highway, the stream abruptly plunges down into a deep cut in solid rock. The sidecanyon on the left here is worth exploring for several miles. Below the grotto, the canyon continues deep and narrow for several more miles before gradually opening out into the broad central canyon. Along this stretch, one major tributary canyon, Hatch Wash, enters from the left, and within the next 3 miles three other lesser sidecanyons join Cane Creek Canyon. Each is worth exploring by those with the time and stamina. The county road penetrates the broadest part of the canyon, but is near the stream course for only the first mile or so of the narrow lower canyon. Within these narrows, Hunter Canyon is another tributary well worth exploring. As the road climbs out of the deep gorge, at the point where a perennial spring gushes out of the cliff, the canyon is again very hikeable on to its confluence with the Colorado River.

NOTES: Cane Creek, or Kane Creek as it is also known, is continuous the length of its canyon in the spring, and for several days following heavy rains, but is generally subsurface or intermittent in the wider part of its gorge at other times. Water flow in Hatch Wash and Hunter Canyon is also seasonal, but some water can be found in them year around. The water in Cane Creek is highly mineralized and may be contaminated by grazing cattle. It should be purified before human use. Hikers should watch for "The Happy Turk" balanced rock near the base of the talus slope below the eastern cliff, about 1 mile north of where the gravel road fords the stream.

Funnel Arch

TYPE OF TRAIL: slickrock.

TRAIL MILEAGE: ½ mile, round trip.

TIME TO HIKE: 1 hour.

U.S.G.S. MAPS: Moab quadrangle.

HAZARDS: hazardous drops.

SEASONS: any season, except when snow is on the ground.

ACCESS: drive downriver from Moab on Cane Creek Road; continue on gravel road into lower Cane Creek Canyon about 2 miles beyond end of pavement; park in pull-out, at top of switchbacks that drop down into canyon; hiking route to Funnel Arch goes up dry watercourse on left of road, opposite pull-out.

TRAIL SUMMARY: The short but steep hike to Funnel Arch provides a close look at a variety of sandstone erosional forms, a beautiful panoramic view of lower Cane Creek Canyon, a visit to graceful Funnel Arch and an access route into a huge expanse of Behind-the-Rocks slickrock country.

TRAIL HIGHLIGHTS

Funnel Arch is a lovely span with an opening of moderate size in a big fin of Navajo sandstone. The arch is on an irregular sand and rock terrace high above lower Cane Creek Canyon, but not far above the gravelled road that penetrates this part of the canyon. The route to the arch begins by ascending a narrow, steep slickrock wash. Shortly, it becomes necessary to climb up a dry waterfall through an eroded cleft in solid rock. Above this, the route follows the watercourse to the right and up a shallow slickrock draw, then out of the draw to the left. From almost any point along the rim of this draw Funnel Arch is visible, just a few hundred feet away, arching down from the sandstone domes and fins that wall the several-acre terrace. Climbing into a large "saddle" between this wall and one rounded dome affords a good view of the gorges below, but a still better view can be had from the top of another nearby dome. The steep, ascending ridge of the sandstone fin just north of Funnel Arch provides access to a whole region of otherwise almost inaccessible slickrock. Only hikers experienced at sandstone free-climbing should attempt this hazardous route.

NOTES: Hikers who plan to go beyond Funnel Arch should take along all the water they will need. Funnel Arch cannot be seen from Cane Creek Road, but is visible from many places on Amasa Back, on the opposite side of Cane Creek Canyon.

Halls Bridge

TYPE OF TRAIL: slickrock.

TRAIL MILEAGE: 1 mile round trip, or more.

TIME TO HIKE: 1 hour round trip, or more.

U.S.G.S. MAPS: Moab quadrangle.

HAZARDS: no water; hazardous drops.

SEASONS: early spring through late fall; not accessible with snow on the ground.

ACCESS: drive down river from Moab on Cane Creek Road to end of pavement; drive or hike off-road vehicle trail up Pritchett Canyon to about 1/8 mile beyond the southern side of Window Arch; drive or hike vehicle trail spur to right toward opposite wall of canyon; follow poorly defined foot trail route up left slopes of large, steep wash just down canyon from end of vehicle trail spur; Halls Bridge is in very large sandstone fin in upper part of this drainage line.

TRAIL SUMMARY: The steep hike to Halls Bridge goes up a picturesque side canyon to the gigantic sandstone fin that contains that very impressive natural span.

TRAIL HIGHLIGHTS

Although Halls Bridge is within sight of the off-road vehicle trail that travels the length of Pritchett Canyon, it stands edgewise to the trail, and is hidden from other viewpoints by sandstone fins on either side. The huge span was first reported in 1911, then apparently forgotten. It was rediscovered by air in 1971. It was then thoroughly photographed, measured, and documented. The hiking route that goes to the "bridge," which is actually an arch, provides excellent views of the span from the narrow sandstone canyon below it, but getting up into the arch's opening is more difficult. There are two routes that can be followed to do this. One ascends a projecting sandstone spur that is below the arch, then follows an obvious route on toward the opening. This route requires free-climbing skills, especially for the trip back down. The other route continues up the narrow canyon to its end, climbs out onto the higher slickrock and sand terraces to the west of Halls Bridge, then returns to the span via another narrow cleft and a sandstone ridge. This route is much longer but is not hazardous. It is possible to climb the rock slopes behind the arch opening up onto the top of the huge span and beyond.

NOTES: Halls Bridge was named after J. Frank Halls, an early cattleman, and is located near the center of the southwestern quarter of the northeastern quarter of Section 26, T 26 S, R 21 E of the Moab quadrangle. A photograph of the span first appeared in the November 17, 1911 edition of the *Grand Valley Times*, but without a story. The two routes to beneath Halls Bridge can also be used to gain access to a large, isolated region of slickrock in Behind-the-Rocks.

Hunter Canyon

TYPE OF TRAIL: canyon-stream.

TRAIL MILEAGE: optional, up to 6 miles round trip, or more.

TIME TO HIKE: optional, up to 5 hours, or more.

U.S.G.S. MAPS: Moab and Hatch Point quadrangles.

HAZARDS: none, within the canyon; hazardous drops if hikers climb above canyon floor.

SEASONS: any season.

ACCESS: drive downriver from Moab on Cane Creek Road; park at mouth of Hunter Canyon, about 3 miles beyond end of pavement.

TRAIL SUMMARY: Lower Hunter Canyon is a well watered tributary of Cane Creek Canyon that is narrow, deep and lovely for the entire 3 miles to the huge spring-fed pool at its box end.

TRAIL HIGHLIGHTS

An intermittent spring-fed stream flows the length of lower Hunter Canyon, offering hikers crystal clear pools, trees, aquatic life, dripping walls and water-loving vegetation at intervals along the narrow canyon floor. Some pools are deep enough to afford a cooling dip during the warmer months. The soaring sandstone walls of the canyon are either very steep or sheer, and in many places are eroded into endless weird shapes and tiny arches. There is a large arch high up on the right wall about 1 mile up the canyon. Another strange span is visible on the same side farther up. The canyon winds and twists for 3 miles before ending in a rock-walled grotto. Seeping springs support a large pool here that is surrounded by rushes and grasses. Where upper Hunter Wash plunges over a dry waterfall above the pool, a small but interesting natural bridge has been cut from the solid rock by eons of flash-flood runoff. A mile-long sidecanyon branches south from Hunter Canyon, not far below the pool. Hikers with free-climbing experience can climb out of lower Hunter Canyon just below the pool on the terraced south wall, if they want access to the upper Hunter Wash and Canyon system, and nearby areas of Behind-the-Rocks.

NOTES: Hikers with the stamina and climbing skills may want to go to Pritchett Arch by going up lower Hunter Canyon, climbing out at its end, following the off-road vehicle trail that crosses Hunter Wash just above the dry waterfall, then hiking beyond the vehicle trail spur to the arch. Retracing this route would be more hazardous than going out via Pritchett Canyon.

Lockhart Basin

TYPE OF TRAIL: canyon-stream.

TRAIL MILEAGE: optional.

TIME TO HIKE: optional.

U.S.G.S. MAPS: Hatch Point, Harts Point, The Needles and Upheaval Dome quadrangles, or map of Canyonlands National Park.

HAZARDS: hazardous drops; remote location; access road impassable or hazardous at times.

SEASONS: best during cooler months of spring or fall, but may be hiked in summer or winter when snow is light.

ACCESS: drive west from U.S. 163 on Utah 211; about 3 miles beyond Indian Creek bridge, turn right onto graded dirt road toward Lockhart Basin; this road will cross drainage lines for Indian Creek, Rustler Canyon, Horsethief Canyon and Lockhart Canyon, plus several tributaries of these, in the next 26 miles.

TRAIL SUMMARY: Hiking down any of the major washes that drain Lockhart Basin and vicinity, to where they join the Colorado River within Canyonlands National Park, will provide an exciting, and sometimes demanding redrock canyon-stream wilderness experience.

TRAIL HIGHLIGHTS

The access road into Lockhart Basin is generally passable to carefully driven highway vehicles, but should not be attempted during, or for a day or two following rain. Similarly, the ford across Indian Creek is not passable to any vehicle during periods of heavy runoff, such as following rain or an early-spring thaw in the higher elevations drained by this stream. Hikers wanting access to the Lockhart Basin canyons during such times can get there via an off-road vehicle trail that leaves Utah 211 about ½ mile east of the Indian Creek bridge, or by hiking cross-country from anywhere before the highway crossed Indian Creek. The several major washes within and south of Lockhart Basin all have much in common, but some are easier to hike than others. Waterfalls, dry and otherwise, are common barriers to easy progress, but these intermittent or seasonal stream courses cut more deeply into the colorful redrock strata, the hike becomes well worth the effort of working around difficult places. Hikers who decide to explore these canyons systematically will find ropes and climbing skills useful. More adventurous hikers may want to try going down Horsethief Canyon to the river, then hiking the riverbank to Lockhart Canyon and out that way.

NOTES: Water found in the Lockhart Basin canyons is highly mineralized, but should be potable with only minor purification. While in the area, hikers will find it rewarding to explore up Harts Draw from the vehicle access road. An off-road vehicle trail goes down the main branch of Lockhart Canyon, to where an old cabin stands near the river.

Pritchett Arch

TYPE OF TRAIL: designated.

TRAIL MILEAGE: 1½ miles, round trip.

TIME TO HIKE: 2 hours, round trip, from nearest off-road vehicle trail; 2 days or more if hiked via Hunter or Pritchett canyons.

U.S.G.S. MAPS: Moab quadrangle.

HAZARDS: no water; hazardous drops; trail poorly marked across stretches of slickrock.

SEASONS: early spring through late fall; not accessible with snow on the ground.

ACCESS: drive downriver from Moab on Cane Creek Road to end of pavement; drive or hike off-road vehicle trail up Pritchett Canyon; after vehicle trail passes spur to Halls Bridge, climbs over a pass and drops into upper Hunter drainage, continue for about 1 mile to short spur trail to the right; follow this trail to its end at the base of a cliff; Pritchett Arch hiking trail starts here.

TRAIL SUMMARY: This highly scenic trail climbs onto a slickrock terrace, goes past one fair-sized arch to reach beautiful Pritchett Arch and two others nearby that do not have official names.

TRAIL HIGHLIGHTS

The hiking trail to Pritchett Arch starts by climbing steeply up onto a broad slickrock terrace, then continues along this terrace as it narrows below a soaring sandstone wall. An oddly shaped arch soon appears in this wall. The view from the terrace is spectacular toward the east. Beyond the complexities of upper Hunter wash, the higher eastern rimlands of Behind the Rocks are topped by the still higher peaks of the La Sal Mountains. A veritable maze of sandstone fins, domes and canyons stretches in all directions. After crossing a small sand flat and a shallow, tree-filled wash, the trail climbs steeply up slickrock slopes toward the north. As this unmarked part of the trail levels out and rounds a corner, the graceful curves of Pritchett Arch appear at the far end of a gigantic rock amphitheater. Trees and bushes grow in the wind-blown, water-washed sand beneath the great span. It is possible to climb part of the way up the sloping, eroded sandstone wall behind the arch. The sheer size and beauty of this outstanding natural span can only be realized by standing directly beneath it. A short walk beyond the span leads to an overlook that offers a view of Window Arch and The Ostrich, an oddly shaped spire in upper Pritchett Canyon, and on down that picturesque canyon. Across a shallow slickrock gully, the big openings of two more arches can be seen in great sandstone masses. One more closely resembles a smoothly rounded tunnel.

NOTES: Hikers who wish to return from Pritchett Arch via Pritchett Canyon should not attempt to descend directly from the arch into the canyon without climbing aids and skills. The safe route follows the vehicle trail. Skilled free-climbers will find it possible but very hazardous to climb up onto Pritchett Arch from behind.

King

Several of us were climbing along the left slopes of a steep, rocky, V-shaped draw high above Pritchett Canyon, heading for Halls Bridge, a huge arch hidden in a gigantic sandstone fin. The going was rough along the slope, but impossible in the boulder-choked wash-bottom, so we were all watching the ground, looking up and ahead only now and then, seeking a first glimpse of the lofty span.

Suddenly, without warning, the man in the lead stopped short, held up a warning hand and said in a hushed but excited voice, "Look, up there!"

We all paused and looked. Just ahead of us a few dozen yards the gully we were climbing ended in a large water-worn amphitheater of solid sandstone. This same slickrock mass extended down the opposite side of the gully to below where we stood. A neat, sheer-walled box-end, with the solid rock wall on down the little canyon only slightly less than vertical.

And there, standing in the rounded alcove at the end of the canyon, within an easy stone's throw, was a magnificent mule deer buck, staring straight at us and frozen into immobility, hoping against all hope that we would not see him.

Ordinarily, his "freeze" defense would have been good in this broken country with its great jagged boulders, sharp and angular shadows and gnarled, twisted juniper trees. But not when he was standing silhouetted against the bright slickrock in that sunny alcove, his statuesque, stately body and branching antlers creating bold bas-relief in both color and form.

For an endless, timeless moment we all stood frozen, staring entranced—the deer at us, and we at him—then the tableau shattered in an explosion of graceful movement as the deer, seeing no other course, bounded in great leaps along the steep slickrock wall just across from us, taking the only route open to him except right through our little group.

He bounded past us like some mythical, magical stag in an ancient, enchanted forest, his sharp hooves seeking and finding tiny ledges and faults in the near-vertical rock wall as he soared down the narrow gulch, passing within scant yards of us as he fled into the open country behind us, back into the vast sandstone maze where he was indisputed king—and leaving behind a small group of intruders into his desert wilderness, still standing enthralled by the majesty of his bearing, and the graceful beauty of his going.

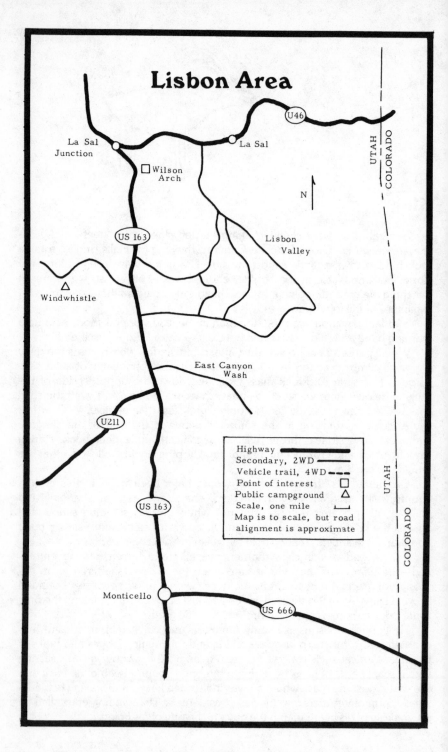

Lisbon Area

La Sal Junction

U46

La Sal

Wilson Arch

N

Lisbon Valley

US 163

△ Windwhistle

East Canyon Wash

U211

US 163

Highway	▅▅▅▅
Secondary, 2WD	▬▬▬
Vehicle trail, 4WD	▬ ▬ ▬
Point of interest	□
Public campground	△
Scale, one mile	⊢⊣

Map is to scale, but road alignment is approximate

UTAH
COLORADO

UTAH
COLORADO

Monticello

US 666

112

Lisbon Area

AREA NAME: This area was named after Lisbon Valley, a 16-mile long valley that angles across the northern part of this area.

AREA BOUNDARIES: U.S. 163, Utah 46, U.S. 666 and Colorado-Utah border.

U.S.G.S. TOPOGRAPHIC MAPS THAT COVER THE AREA: La Sal Junction, La Sal, Lisbon Valley, Hatch Rock, Eastland and Monticello quadrangles.

GENERAL TOPOGRAPHY: west-central area is broad sandflats terminated by meandering slickrock walls and set with isolated outcroppings of the same rock; higher ground to the north, east and south consisting of newer, less spectacular formations cut by shallow valleys and canyons, mostly covered with pinyon-juniper forests and related vegetation.

SUGGESTED BASE CAMPS: motels or commercial campgrounds in Moab or Monticello; developed public campgrounds at Newspaper Rock State Historical Monument and in Canyon Rims Recreation Area; primitive camping is permitted almost anywhere within the area except on private or leased property, which is generally posted.

ACCESS ROUTES: U.S. 163, U.S. 666, Utah 46, county roads and off-road vehicle trails as shown on the area map.

AREA NOTES:
1. The non-designated hiking trails, routes and areas listed are just representative samples of the primitive hiking available in this area.
2. There is considerable old and current mineral search, extraction and refining activity in the central part of this area. Hikers would be well advised to avoid such activity.
3. The relatively level highlands in the southern part of this area are largely private property and under cultivation.

East Canyon Wash

TYPE OF TRAIL: canyon rim.

TRAIL MILEAGE: optional, up to 10 miles or more.

TIME TO HIKE:optional, up to 2 days or more.

U.S.G.S. MAPS: Lisbon Valley and Hatch Rock quadrangles.

HAZARDS: no water; hazardous cliffs.

SEASONS: best during cooler months of spring or fall, but may be hiked in summer.

ACCESS: drive on U.S. 163 to about 1½ miles north of Utah 211 junction; turn east on graded dirt road; road travels broad lower stretch of East Canyon Wash and provides access to canyon rims on foot or via several off-road vehicle trails.

TRAIL SUMMARY: Hiking the broken rimlands of East Canyon Wash provides a continuous panoramic view, excellent rockhounding and a chance to see several natural and historic highlights within and at the base of the beautiful sandstone cliffs that wall much of the valley.

TRAIL HIGHLIGHTS

East Canyon Wash was once the route of an 1870s exploring party that left Santa Fe, New Mexico, with a goal of reaching the confluence of the Colorado and Green rivers. The report on that early expedition into the canyon country of what was to become southeastern Utah described the colorful Entrada sandstone cliffs of the broad lower 10 miles of East Canyon, which is called East Canyon Wash. The rim of this long, meandering canyon wall can provide a delightful but challenging hiking route for those also interested in rockhounding, because the geologic strata that form ascending terraces above the slickrock rim are rich in fossils and mineral specimens. There are also attractions within and below the convoluted sandstone cliffs. One huge alcove, about 2 miles in from the canyon mouth on the north wall, contains a beautiful arch. Not far upcanyon near the same wall is an old, abandoned ranch. Another mile or so upcanyon, a log corral is built out from a natural rock overhang that is near a huge water-formed cavern. The rimlands and base of East Canyon Wash offer many other such interesting natural and human history sites. The road into the canyon provides easy access up the southern rim, and the rockhounding there is good, but the north rim provides the most spectacular and challenging route. This rim can be easily reached at the narrow upper end of East Canyon Wash. Hikers with free-climbing skills will find other routes up the cliff at intervals. The north rim can also be followed beyond the mouth of the canyon, north and east into Dry Wash, where other roads and vehicle trails provide convenient egress, and the panoramic views to the north are outstanding.

NOTES: Hiking along the base of the Entrada sandstone cliffs that form the north wall of East Canyon Wash and on into Dry Wash can be quite rewarding, although rockhounding will be minimal. Hikers with the time and stamina might like to start at the narrower upper end of the wash, follow the Entrada rim around Deer Neck Mesa into Dry Wash, then back along the cliff base, thus sampling all that this fascinating cliff line has to offer.

Hook & Ladder Gulch

TYPE OF TRAIL: slickrock.

TRAIL MILEAGE: optional.

TIME TO HIKE: optional, up to 2 days.

U.S.G.S. MAPS: Hatch Rock quadrangle.

HAZARDS: no water; hazardous drops.

SEASONS: best during cooler months of spring or fall, but may be hiked in summer, or winter when snow is light.

ACCESS: drive on U.S. 163 to about 3 miles south of Wilson Arch; off-road vehicle trail through gate in highway fence provides easy access into hiking area.

TRAIL SUMMARY: Hiking the area of Hook & Ladder Gulch and its many short tributary canyons provides an intimate look at several square miles of colorful, intricately eroded Entrada sandstone walls, slopes, arches, caves, domes and fins, below higher terraces of younger deposits.

TRAIL HIGHLIGHTS

Hiking the Hook & Ladder vicinity is essentially freestyle exploration of a fascinatingly complex and beautiful maze of salmon-hued slickrock, twisting dry washes and sand dunes held in place by cryptogamic soil and thriving pinyon and juniper trees and other desert vegetation. One shallow wash near the highway contains the filled-in remnants of an old CCC rock-and-wire "reservoir." A small but lovely natural span called Lopez Arch is visible from the highway. It is possible to climb up beneath this opening on its east side, and even closer on the west. A few rarely used off-road vehicle trails penetrate the canyon system to a minor extent, but hikers can either use them for convenient access, or easily avoid them entirely. Hikers who are alert will see many indications of wildlife in this primitive area, and rockhounds will find the layered deposits above the dominant slickrock to be worth exploring. Some specimens may be found on slickrock terraces, where they have fallen from above.

NOTES: This area is attractive in that it can be reached by paved road. Hikers lacking off-road vehicles can park just through the highway fence gate and be quite close to a very primitive and beautiful area. The highway fence is for cattle control. Close the gate after entering.

Wilson Canyon

TYPE OF TRAIL: canyon-stream.

TRAIL MILEAGE: optional, up to 4 miles round trip or more.

TIME TO HIKE: optional, up to 2 days or more.

U.S.G.S. MAPS: La Sal Junction quadrangle.

HAZARDS: water should be purified; hazardous drops above wash bottom.

SEASONS: best during cooler months of spring or fall, but may be hiked in summer, or winter when snow is light.

ACCESS: drive on U.S. 163 to where highway crosses major wash 1½ miles south of Wilson Arch; hike up wash into Wilson Canyon; for closer access, off-road vehicle trails go through gates in highway fence to north and south of wash.

TRAIL SUMMARY: Wilson Canyon is a short but exceptionally beautiful Entrada sandstone gorge that offers good rockhounding, picturesque spires, an unusual natural bridge and some erosional forms not found in other canyons in this area.

TRAIL HIGHLIGHTS

The wash that drains Wilson Canyon goes under the highway after winding through a mile of rolling sand flats. The bottom of the wash is alternately sand and slickrock, with dry waterfalls, ledges and potholes along the way. As the wash approaches the colorful Entrada sandstone cliffs of Wilson Canyon, it deepens, cutting sharply into still

116

older Navajo sandstone and creating a deep, narrow inner gorge within the wider canyon. Broad, rocky terraces studded with trees and brush extend from the main inner gorge to the bases of the towering, salmon-hued cliffs. Convolutions in these cliffs leave picturesque, protruding ridges and spires set among echoing amphitheaters and deep alcoves. The inner gorge has several tributaries worth exploring, but none cut so deeply into the white Navajo sandstone. Most contain lovely erosional forms and potholes, some with water most of the time. The main inner gorge is well worth hiking to its upper end before exploring its branches and the intermediate levels in the canyon. Pools of water fill the gorge as the steep walls close in, forcing hikers to either wade or turn back. Those who persist will be rewarded by reaching a small natural bridge of unusual shape. Where the water course first cuts deeply into the Navajo sandstone, eons of sporadic flow has polished an almost vertical shute, and drilled a great hole into the solid rock near the base of that shute. This deep, narrow pothole eventually broke through at the bottom, leaving a high, thin-walled natural bridge. It is possible to climb under and beyond this bridge, but not on up the shute without aid from above. Surrounding the inner gorge, along the base of the Entrada cliffs, a fairly thin exposure of dark red Dewey Bridge siltstone contains quantities of chert and agate. Chunks of these hard minerals are left lying around as the softer material erodes away.

NOTES: The highway fences are for cattle control. Always close gates. Deer are often seen in this box-end canyon system, and other wildlife also depends upon the water in its perennial springs and deep potholes. In the spring and early summer the water just below the little natural bridge is chest deep and very cold. The water level may be lower later in the season.

Wilson Rims

TYPE OF TRAIL: canyon rim.

TRAIL MILEAGE: about 6 miles.

TIME TO HIKE: 1 day.

U.S.G.S. MAPS: La Sal Junction quadrangle.

HAZARDS: no water; hazardous cliffs.

SEASONS: best during cooler months of spring or fall, but may be hiked in summer.

ACCESS: drive on U.S. 163 to vicinity of Wilson Arch, about 3 miles south of La Sal Junction; access points to Wilson rimlands are from the highway, just north of Wilson Arch, and from about 1½ miles south of Wilson Arch, immediately south of where highway crosses Wilson Canyon wash.

TRAIL SUMMARY: This hiking route climbs onto the high sandstone rim that defines the beautiful Wilson Canyon system, and affords breathtaking views of these colorful, unspoiled canyons, Wilson Arch from above, and broad panoramas of the exceptionally scenic country to the north, south and west.

TRAIL HIGHLIGHTS

This beautiful hiking route can be traveled in either direction. From the south, it leaves the highway at or near where an off-road vehicle trail goes through the highway fence, goes east across the meadows toward the sandstone bluffs, then takes any route practical up the sloping slickrock ridges there to the high Entrada sandstone wall that heads eastward around Wilson Canyon. The route stays on or near the rim, offering endless breathtaking views down into the canyon, and good rockhounding in the higher strata. Farther on, the rim route approaches the highway, then retreats eastward again to skirt another great, rock-walled alcove, offering unusual views of huge Wilson Arch to the west. The route can end just north of this arch, where it is fairly easy to get down slickrock slopes to the highway, or it can continue northward to connect with an off-road vehicle trail that gives access to Utah 46.

NOTES: Free-climbing skills may be desirable on this hiking route, depending upon where the rim is approached and left.

History in the Raw

We were poking among the tumbled-down ruins of an old shack near a long-abandoned mine in a remote canyon. Dark, sand-blasted boards lay around, pierced with the square nails that collectors love. Old machinery stood nearby, rusted into a solid mass except for its smooth bronze bearings.

Not a single wall of the old cabin still stood. The fallen boards were in tangled heaps, like giant jackstraws, protecting bits of trash and personal effects left by its long-ago occupants.

Old shoes, their leather curled and stiff from exposure, told that at least one man and one woman had called the crude shack home.

As I puzzled over scattered pieces of mining machinery, my wife poked around in the collapsed dwelling. A few minutes later she approached me as I peered cautiously down a dark, crumbling mine shaft.

"Look what I found under a board." She handed me a weathered envelope, its corners rotted and flaking.

"Don't open it here — it would fall to pieces," I warned.

Back home that evening, we examined the envelope more closely, wondering what bit of personal history it might reveal, what tale it might tell about the romantic, pioneering past of a canyon country then hardly known to the outside world. The ink on the envelope's surface had long since faded to invisibility, protecting the mystery of its contents.

Carefully, we steamed the envelope open at its seams, then just as carefully moistened the two crumbling sheets of paper it contained. Bit by bit, we opened each fragile, rotten sheet, placing bits and pieces on a slab of cardboard like a jigsaw puzzle.

Parts of each were rotted away, but enough was left to make out all the important details.

The sheets were form letters, with blanks to be filled in by the sender. The ink in the blanks was a faded brown, but still legible, and these faint markings told that in some ways not much has changed as our nation has matured.

The forms were notices from a collection agency that claimed to be "the most extensive Protection and Collection Agency in the country." There were two forms, one for a man, one for his wife. Each was "notice 5," which spoke of a growing desperation on the part of the agency.

In addition to the usual list of pompous threats to use "extreme measures" to collect the amounts due unless payment was made "at once," the forms listed in their blanks the names of the "irresponsible persons," the items they had purchased on credit and the money due.

The woman was being dunned for her credit purchase of "Colliers Weekly" for the sum of "$1.20." Her husband owed "$8.60" for a "dictionary and notions."

The collection forms were evidently printed for use in the first decade of the twentieth century, because there was only room for one digit after the printed numerals, "190." The full date on the two forms was "June 16, 1904."

And, despite their somewhat stilted, archaic language, the forms could still be used today. That's progress?

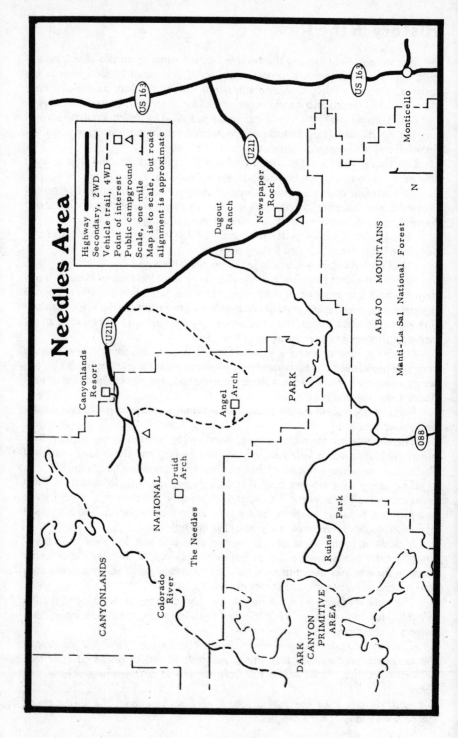

Needles Area

Highway
Secondary, 2WD
Vehicle trail, 4WD
Point of interest □
Public campground △
Scale, one mile
Map is to scale, but road alignment is approximate

US 163

U211

Dugout Ranch

Newspaper Rock

Monticello

N

ABAJO MOUNTAINS

Manti-La Sal National Forest

U211

Canyonlands Resort

Angel Arch

PARK

088

NATIONAL

Druid Arch

The Needles

Ruins Park

Colorado River

CANYONLANDS

DARK CANYON PRIMITIVE AREA

Needles Area

AREA NAME: This area was named after the Needles District of Canyonlands National Park which dominates the western part of the area.

AREA BOUNDARIES: U.S. 163, Utah 211 and its extension in Canyonlands National Park, the Colorado River, the northeastern boundary of the Dark Canyon Primitive Area and the northern National Forest boundary of the Abajo Mountains.

U.S.G.S. TOPOGRAPHIC MAPS THAT COVER THE AREA: The Needles, Harts Point, Mt. Linnaeus, Fable Valley, Monticello, Hatch Rock and map of Canyonlands National Park.

GENERAL TOPOGRAPHY: wooded mesalands in the south, cut by long, twisting and very picturesque canyon systems that flow generally northward; a unique sandstone wilderness of colorful spires, ridges, "grabens," domes, gorges and open sandflats in the Needles area of the park; open redrock country, deep canyons and open sandflats to the east.

SUGGESTED BASE CAMPS: motels or commercial campgrounds in Monticello; developed public campgrounds in the Needles District of Canyonlands National Park and at Newspaper Rock State Historical Monument; primitive campgrounds as designated in the park, and primitive camping almost anywhere outside of the park except on the private ranchlands in lower Indian Creek Canyon.

ACCESS ROUTES: Utah 211, county and park roads and off-road vehicle trails as shown on the area map.

AREA NOTES:
1.   The non-designated hiking trails, routes and areas listed are just representative samples of the primitive hiking available in this area.
2.   Park Service maps, brochures and trail guides give details about roads, hiking and vehicle trails, primitive camping and scenic highlights within the Needles District of Canyonlands National Park. For unpublished changes and additions to such literature, contact park rangers.

3.   The canyons in this area are exceptionally colorful with wild-flowers in the spring, especially following wet winters, and with still other wildflowers and deciduous foliage in the fall.

4.   Hikers should bear in mind that all the numerous archeological sites in this area are protected by Federal law, whether in the park or on the surrounding federal land.

5.   As a safety precaution, the Park Service requires that hikers obtain backcountry permits before taking any of the park trails.

Big Spring - Confluence

TYPE OF TRAIL: designated.

TRAIL MILEAGE: 10 miles, round trip.

TIME TO HIKE: 1 day.

U.S.G.S. MAPS: The Needles quadrangle, or map of Canyonlands National Park.

HAZARDS: water only at river; hazardous drops.

SEASONS: best during cooler months of spring or fall, but may be hiked in summer or winter when snow is light.

ACCESS: drive into Canyonlands National Park on Utah 211; continue on paved park road to Big Spring Canyon; hiking trail begins here.

TRAIL SUMMARY: This picturesque trail to the overlook above the confluence of the Green and Colorado rivers gives hikers an excellent look at some of the wild canyon and slickrock country in the Needles District of Canyonlands National Park.

TRAIL HIGHLIGHTS

The trail to the Confluence of the Green and Colorado Rivers begins by crossing deep and picturesque Big Spring Canyon. For the next couple of miles, it winds through very broken but scenic slickrock country to lower Elephant Canyon. The trail then drops into this beautiful gorge, follows it for a short distance then climbs out to continue through more highlands to meet and cross an off-road vehicle trail, then on to Confluence Overlook. Both of the big canyons crossed by the trail are excellent examples of the many canyons in this area that cut into layered Cedar Mesa sandstone and the colorful rock strata below. The higher stretches of the trail wind through mazes of eroded Cedar Mesa, and near the end of the trail, where it parallels the vehicle trail, hikers get views down Cyclone Canyon, one of the many "grabens," or long, rock-

walled valleys, in the Needles. The Confluence Overlook provides a breathtaking view down into the Colorado River gorge, where it is joined by the equally spectacular Green River gorge. The rivers at this point are almost 1000 feet below the viewpoint.

NOTES: It is possible, and very rewarding, to hike both up and down Big Spring and Elephant canyons from where the trail crosses these deep, narrow gorges. See Park Service maps for connections with the vehicle trail and other hiking trails via Elephant Canyon. Backpackers may want to hike this trail to the Confluence, then down Cyclone Canyon to connect with other Needles area trails.

Davis Canyon

TYPE OF TRAIL: canyon-stream.

TRAIL MILEAGE: optional.

TIME TO HIKE: optional, up to several days.

U.S.G.S. MAPS: Harts Point, or map of Canyonlands National Park.

HAZARDS: hazardous drops in vicinity of arches and archeological sites.

SEASONS: best during cooler months of spring or fall, but may be hiked in summer, or winter when snow is light.

ACCESS: drive west on Utah 211 from U.S. 163; continue down Indian Creek Canyon into open country; immediately beyond Indian Creek bridge, an off-road vehicle trail goes left; drive or hike this trail into Davis Canyon.

TRAIL SUMMARY: Davis Canyon is a magnificent, branching canyon system that offers hikers endless opportunities to explore these canyons and see numerous arches, Indian ruins and other archeological sites.

TRAIL HIGHLIGHTS

The off-road vehicle trail that approaches and enters Davis Canyon travels mostly in the wash bottom and provides a convenient access route for hikers. As the canyon deepens and narrows, the vehicle trail is confined to the wash bottom of the main canyon and a very few of its major tributaries, leaving many miles of exceptionally lovely and primitive canyons that can be explored only on foot. Topographic maps show the locations of a few of the arches and ruins in this complex canyon system, but there are many more. New discoveries are still being made in this and other nearby canyons. Hikers who wish to spend several days or more exploring Davis Canyon will find an excellent primitive camping area beside a trickling stream under some cottonwoods right at the park boundary. Other sources of water in this canyon system can be found up various side-canyons. One such canyon has a rare log structure set among other rock dwellings high on a ledge. Another side-canyon has a beautiful granary under an arch. Locating such unusual archaeological sites is part of the fun of exploring Davis Canyon.

NOTES: Hikers who want to see Davis Canyon in all its spring finery, and before much visitation by off-road vehicles, should plan to visit the canyon prior to Easter. Autumn trips, in October, are also rewarding, but water may be less available. Hiking up to some of the arches and ruins in Davis Canyon provides free-climbing opportunities, but can be very hazardous. The nearby Lavender Canyon complex is similar to

Davis Canyon, but much longer, and with more and larger arches and Indian ruins. It is considerably farther from the highway to Lavender, making an off-road vehicle desirable for access. There is generally potable water available many places within Lavender and its branches.

Druid Arch

TYPE OF TRAIL: designated.

TRAIL MILEAGE: 11 miles, round trip, Elephant Hill to Druid Arch; other routes vary.

TIME TO HIKE: 1 day, from Elephant Hill; longer via trail from campground.

U.S.G.S. MAPS: The Needles quadrangle, or map of Canyonlands National Park.

HAZARDS: water only in upper Elephant Canyon; hazardous drops near trails and in vicinity of arch.

SEASONS: best during cooler months of spring or fall, but may be hiked in summer.

ACCESS: drive west on Utah 211 from U.S. 163 into Canyonlands National Park; continue on paved park road to Squaw Flat campground; one trail begins here; for access via Elephant Hill, drive on to Elephant Hill on graded dirt road; hiking trailhead is at base of "hill"; for other access routes, drive or hike off-road vehicle trail over Elephant Hill and on to Devils Kitchen campground; Park Service trail maps show several routes from here to Druid Arch.

TRAIL SUMMARY: All of the trails that approach unique Druid Arch eventually travel upper Elephant Canyon with its soaring, spectacular walls, and all approaches wind through the beautiful and colorful erosional forms of Cedar Mesa sandstone that give the Needles area its name.

TRAIL HIGHLIGHTS

The trail from Elephant Hill begins at the base of that tortuous stretch of off-road vehicle trail, climbs steeply up into colorful masses of eroded sandstone, crosses slickrock and sand flats to drop down into picturesque Elephant Canyon for the last several miles. A short spur trail offers breathtaking views down into and beyond Elephant Canyon from the vantage point of shaded canyon-rim caverns. Three other trail routes that start at the Devils Kitchen campground wind through soaring "needles" of rock, then cross the lovely meadows of Chesler Park before dropping into Elephant Canyon. The longest route, from the Squaw Flat campground, offers two approaches. Both climb great slickrock ridges and masses, and cross other canyon systems, before descending into upper Elephant Canyon. Druid Arch is formed by great vertical slabs of rock that are topped by a caprock, making an "arch" of two vertical openings, one large, the other barely more than a slit. The span stands on a sandstone ridge in the upper end of Elephant Canyon. Hiking around the base of the towering arch offers challenges and hazards. The size of this unusual natural span can only be appreciated from directly below. The arch somewhat resembles the great stone slabs of Stonehenge.

NOTES: Hikers who want to spend some time around Druid Arch, especially photographers who need varied lighting, should plan to camp nearby overnight.

Joint Trail

TYPE OF TRAIL: designated.

TRAIL MILEAGE: 2 miles, round trip, from off-road vehicle trailhead.

TIME TO HIKE: 2 hours, round trip.

U.S.G.S. MAPS: The Needles quadrangle, or map of Canyonlands National Park.

HAZARDS: this trail is not for claustrophobic hikers.

SEASONS: early spring through late fall, but may also be hiked winter when snow is light.

ACCESS: drive west on Utah 211 from U.S. 163 into Canyonlands National Park; continue on paved park road to Squaw Flat campground; for access to Joint Trail via other hiking trails, follow designated trails from campground to south side of Chesler Park and on through Joint Trail; for access via off-road vehicle trail to head of Joint Trail, drive from campground to Elephant Hill on graded dirt road; drive or hike off-road vehicle trail over Elephant Hill and beyond to Chesler Canyon; hiking trailhead is here.

TRAIL SUMMARY: The Joint Trail offers hikers an experience that can be had few other places in the country, as the trail goes through huge echoing caverns and extremely narrow crevices in great masses of sandstone, to arrive at a viewpoint overlooking lovely Chesler Park.

TRAIL HIGHLIGHTS

The most dramatic approach to the Joint Trail and Chesler Park is via the off-road vehicle trail that goes up Chesler Canyon. From the parking area at the head of the Joint Trail, the hiking trail first climbs the forested, rocky slopes of Chesler Canyon, offering enchanting views of the "needles" in the near-distance. Soon, the trail enters a series of vast, echoing caverns formed by water erosion beneath great masses of solid Cedar Mesa sandstone. These shadowed caverns offer a cool respite from the sun during the warmer months. The trail next enters a long stretch of connecting "joints," or deep, narrow crevices in the immense bulk of sandstone that rings Chesler Park. Some of these crevices are only 3 or 4 feet apart, and branching cracks are even narrower. The trail finally climbs steeply out of one crevice and up a series of slickrock slopes and steps to a viewpoint overlooking Chesler Park, with its broad, open meadows surrounded on all sides by a towering wall of banded sandstone spires, fins and ridges. Near this overlook, other foot trails cross Chesler Park. One heads toward Elephant Canyon and can be used as a route to Druid Arch. Hiking back through the Joint Trail offers still other perspectives on this strangely beautiful hiking route that has been created by eons of erosion, with just a little help from the National Park Service.

NOTES: The hike to Druid Arch from the Chesler Canyon off-road vehicle trail, via the Joint Trail and Chesler Park, is about 9½ miles round trip.

Red Lake Canyon

TYPE OF TRAIL: designated.

TRAIL MILEAGE: 8 miles round trip from the Cyclone Canyon trailhead.

TIME TO HIKE: 1 day or more.

U.S.G.S. MAPS: The Needles quadrangle, or map of Canyonlands National Park.

HAZARDS: steep grades; hazardous drops; very dangerous river.

SEASONS: best during cooler months of spring or fall, but may be hiked in summer.

ACCESS: drive west on Utah 211 from U.S. 163 into Canyonlands National Park; continue on paved park road to Squaw Flat campground; drive on graded dirt road to Elephant Hill; drive or hike off-road vehicle trail over Elephant Hill and beyond into Cyclone Canyon; head of hiking trail down Lower Red Lake Canyon begins here.

TRAIL SUMMARY: This demanding trail offers hikers a good look at the "Grabens" area of the Needles District of Canyonlands National Park before descending steeply down into the Colorado River gorge to the river, 3½ miles downstream from the Green-Colorado confluence, but still almost a mile above the first rapid in Cataract Canyon.

TRAIL HIGHLIGHTS

The hiking trail down Lower Red Lake Canyon begins by climbing through the slickrock wall that separates Cyclone Canyon from still another "graben," Upper Red Lake Canyon. From there, the trail descends very steeply down the slopes of Lower Red Lake Canyon, eventually to reach a river bottomland. One stretch of this trail drops 700 feet in less than ½ mile. It is possible to hike downstream along the river bank to the upper rapids of Cataract Canyon. Those who wish to camp overnight will find sites along the river. The rock formations high on the opposite rivergorge rim are called "The Dollhouse." Although a foot trail climbs from the opposite river bottom to the Dollhouse, and connects with a series of other trails in the Maze District of the park, hikers should not attempt to cross the river here by any means but a boat.

NOTES: The trail down Lower Red Lake Canyon and back out is very demanding, and should be attempted only by hikers in good physical condition. The only water available on this trail is at the river. River water should be boiled, settled and chemically purified before drinking. Even then its soluble mineral content will be high. Strong currents make swimming in the Colorado River extremely dangerous. "Graben" means "grave." The long, sunken valleys in this part of the park are reminiscent of old, sunken graves.

Salt Creek Canyon

TYPE OF TRAIL: designated.

TRAIL MILEAGE: 28 miles one way; add 13 miles for round trip up Horse Canyon; 12 miles one way down primitive upper Salt Creek Canyon, if coordinated with an off-road vehicle in lower canyon.

TIME TO HIKE: optional, 2 days or more.

U.S.G.S. MAPS: The Needles, Harts Point, Mt. Linnaeus and Fable Valley quadrangles, or map of Canyonlands National Park.

HAZARDS: upper canyon very remote.

SEASONS: best during cooler months of spring or fall, but may be hiked in summer or winter when snow is light.

ACCESS: For access at lower end of canyon, drive west on Utah 211 from U.S. 163 into Canyonlands National Park; continue on paved park road to spur road to Cave Spring; near Cave Spring, drive or hike off-road vehicle trail up Salt Creek Canyon; for access at upper end of canyon, drive west on Utah 211 from U.S. 163 to Dugout Ranch; turn left on rough graded dirt road up North Cottonwood Canyon; after 3 miles, take fork right across creek, then continue toward Cathedral

Butte; hiking trail into upper Salt Creek Canyon begins at vehicle trail about ¼ mile beyond nearest approach to Cathedral Butte.

TRAIL SUMMARY: The trail down long and winding Salt Creek Canyon provides backpackers an intimate look at one of the most beautiful wilderness areas in Canyonlands National Park, with many large arches, historic and prehistoric sites and optional side trips to famous Angel Arch and up the Horse Canyon tributary to still other archeological sites and large arches.

TRAIL HIGHLIGHTS

Salt Creek goes through a lot of spectacularly beautiful and varied canyon country in its journey from the Abajo Mountain foothills to the Colorado River. Along this twisting route this intermittent, seasonal stream flows through four distinctive types of terrain; wooded mountains; a twisting, sandstone canyon with eroded, convoluted walls; open desert; and a deep, colorful gorge. The second and longest stretch of Salt Creek, the picturesque wilderness canyon that begins at the southern park boundary and ends near Cave Spring, offers the best hiking. This long canyon is joined by several major and many minor tributaries as it winds and twists between mile after mile of colorful, banded Cedar Mesa sandstone walls. The main canyon can be hiked in either direction, with worthwhile side trips encountered along its entire length. Backpackers could easily spend a week or more exploring the many features of upper Salt Creek Canyon and its tributaries. Beginning at the dirt road just south of the park boundary, the foot trail drops abruptly into one upper arm of the canyon. As an alternate approach route, those who enjoy rim-hiking will find it worthwhile to hike out along the western rim of the slender, elevated peninsula that projects into the park between upper Salt Creek and upper Lavender canyons. This peninsula rim affords excellent views down into both of these canyons. From near its tip, it is possible to spot three arches, several Indian ruins and Kirk's Cabin, all in Salt Creek Canyon. With a little effort, one can hike down from the tip of this peninsula into Big Pocket, a broad, meadowed arm of Salt Creek Canyon that has many ruins in its alcoved walls. On down the main canyon, many side canyons lure hikers, and arches beckon from high in the rounded sandstone walls. About 7½ miles down the main canyon, a short spur trail goes to an exquisite pictograph called the "All-American Man," because of its red, white and blue colors. The next major feature is the Upper Jump, where the trickling stream cascades down a series of rock ledges. Not far below this is the end of the washbottom off-road vehicle trail that penetrates the lower canyon, and just a little farther down a side canyon gives access to the trail to Angel Arch. About 8½ miles beyond this turnoff, a spur foot trail heads west from the Peekaboo Springs primitive campsite to join a whole system of trails in the Squaw Flat-Needles area of the park. In about another mile, Horse Canyon branches off. Although an off-road vehicle trail penetrates this canyon too for some distance, hikers will find plenty there worth exploring, including Paul Bunyan's Potty, Tower Ruin, several major arches and a number of other archeological sites. The last couple of miles below the Salt Creek-Horse Canyon confluence cross open desert-wash country that is set among low, rounded domes and walls of sandstone.

NOTES: Backpackers can normally expect to find enough potable water in upper Salt Creek Canyon and its tributaries to permit lengthy camping, although some water may be highly mineralized. Hikers who persist can find an unmarked hiking route from the popular viewpoint of Angel Arch near The Molar, to beneath and behind this immense span. This climb is well worth the time and effort it takes. Hikers who prefer to avoid off-road vehicles along the trails in Horse Canyon and lower Salt Creek Canyon should plan their trips either before or after the main tourist season, that is, before Memorial Day or after Labor Day. The canyon is usually hikeable as early as March or April, depending on the year's weather, and through November some years.

Squaw Flat Trails

TYPE OF TRAILS: designated.

TRAIL MILEAGE: optional.

TIME TO HIKE: optional.

U.S.G.S. MAPS: The Needles quadrangle, or map of Canyonlands National Park.

HAZARDS: limited water; hazardous drops.

ACCESS: drive west on Utah 211 from U.S. 163 into Canyonlands National Park; continue on paved park road to Squaw Flat campground; various hiking trails begin at or near the campground, at the base of Elephant Hill 3 miles west, or from Peekaboo Spring, 3½ miles up Salt Creek from Cave Spring vicinity.

TRAIL SUMMARY: The interconnecting system of hiking trails in the Squaw Flat-Needles area of Canyonlands National Park offers hikers an intimate look at the primitive and unspoiled "needles" country that is a unique and beautiful part of this park.

TRAIL HIGHLIGHTS

Every mile of the many interconnecting trails in the Needles District of Canyonlands National Park is worth hiking. The trails cross or travel in deep and lovely canyons, climb across or follow high ridges of

eroded sandstone, wind and twist through mazes of rock spires and narrow crevices and meander across beautiful, grassy "parks" surrounded by soaring, banded fingers of ancient stone. The variety of sandstone erosional forms encountered is endless, with soaring "needles," great arches, vast caverns, echoing alcoves, age-streaked walls and great, rounded domes being the most outstanding. In the canyons where there is, or once was water, archeological sites abound, and in some places there are remnants of such historical, pre-park uses of the area as ranching and mining. Some of the earlier vehicle trails created by prospectors have been closed and restored, but others have been retained to permit some limited vehicular access into this wild and broken region. These terribly rough "jeep trails" are, themselves, historic remnants of an earlier time. Such trails can be used by hikers to gain access into areas otherwise very difficult to reach. Although the primary access points for the Squaw Flat-Needles hiking trail system are at or near Squaw Flat, it is possible to enter or leave the system via Salt Creek Canyon, or via the off-road vehicle trail up Bobbys Hole to Ruin Park and Beef Basin. The designated foot trail system also provides access to other primitive hiking routes within the Needles District and out to the south and southwest. Such routes through the wilderness areas of the park and on south should be attempted only by experienced, well-prepared backpackers.

NOTES: The Park Service issues a small trail map of the Needles District, and a booklet listing details about most of the designated trails there, including a few water sources. Day hikers will find that the Devils Kitchen primitive campground makes a good base camp. The Squaw Flat campground is generally full during the main tourist season. Park rangers are usually willing to suggest good wilderness hiking routes.

134

Pinkie

My wife and I were returning up the badly eroded vehicle trail from an old uranium mine just below the rim of the slender, elevated peninsula of land that separates upper Salt Creek and Lavender Canyons at the southern boundary of Canyonlands National Park. We had dubbed the skinny mesa "Big Pocket Overlook" because of the marvelous views from its tip down into Big Pocket, a broad, slickrock-walled side-canyon to Salt Creek Canyon that contains many ancient Anasazi Indian structures.

As we threaded our way among the bushes, boulders and gullies on the mine trail, we discussed a curious thing about the long-abandoned mine. It had the usual desert-weathered timbers outside the mine's mouth in the ore shute and related structures, but just inside the mine, one of the timbers used to support the crumbling mine roof was a horizontal petrified log, still in its convenient original position within the mine-shaft ceiling.

My wife, who was walking a few feet behind me, suddenly stopped and said "Listen!" I did, but heard nothing. My hearing is less acute than hers. Slowly, she inched forward, sonaring in on what she had heard beside the trail. I did the same, guided by her movements, knowing by then what she must have heard.

Sure enough, there he was, coiled up fearfully against the bluff face, trying to look invisible but rattling his tiny castanets in a warning buzz — an adult midget faded rattler, only slightly more than two feet long. I had walked right by him, the noise of my own progress through the bushes masking his strident, high-pitched alarm.

His color was one we had never seen. Most of this rare midget species are a pale, washed-out beige in color, hence their common name. This one, however, had a distinct reddish hue overlying the usual faint, mottled markings. He was a pale brick-red.

Using a sturdy twig from a nearby shrub, I slowly, gently picked up our nervous friend. Oddly, he gripped the stick tightly with the last few inches of his tail, like one of the larger constrictors. And there he hung, hissing his tiny heart out, but unable to vibrate his tail-tip, while my wife took his picture at close range.

After we had marveled a few more moments at this oddity among rarities, I gently set the sinuous little fellow down beside some bushes on the down-slope side of the trail and said, "get along out of sight, before someone sees you who doesn't like snakes." He did.

135

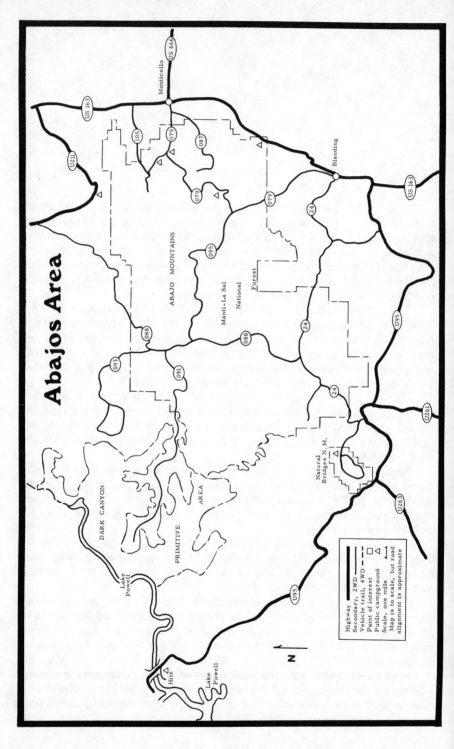

Abajos Area

Highway, 2WD
Secondary, 2WD
Vehicle trail, 4WD
Point of interest □
Public campground △
Scale, one mile
Map is to scale, but road
alignment is approximate

N

136

Abajos Area

AREA NAME: This area was named after the Abajo Mountains which dominate this section of the Manti-La Sal National Forest and the surrounding foothills.

AREA BOUNDARIES: The northern National Forest boundary, U.S. 163, Utah 95, the Colorado River gorge and the northern boundary of the Dark Canyon Primitive Area.

U.S.G.S. TOPOGRAPHIC MAPS THAT COVER THE AREA: Monticello, Mt. Linnaeus, Fable Valley, Mouth of Dark Canyon, Natural Bridges, Bears Ears, Brushy Basin, Blanding, Mancos Mesa, Browns Rim, The Needles and Orange Cliffs quadrangles.

GENERAL TOPOGRAPHY: mountains with peaks up to 11,360 feet elevation, surrounded by broad, sloping sedimentary strata that are cut by deep drainage lines to form mesas, slender peninsulas and deep, winding canyon systems radiating east, south and west from the mountains.

SUGGESTED BASE CAMPS: motels and commercial campgrounds in Monticello and Blanding; developed public campgrounds in the Needles District of Canyonlands National Park, at Newspaper Rock State Historical Monument, at Natural Bridges National Monument, at Hite Marina on Lake Powell and at Devils Canyon, Red Bluff, Dalton Springs and Buckboard within the National Forest; primitive camping is permitted almost anywhere within the National Forest and surrounding areas except on private property, which is usually posted, or within Natural Bridges National Monument or Canyonlands National Park; contact park rangers for current regulations there.

ACCESS ROUTES: U.S. 163, Utah 211, Utah 95, county and Forest Service roads and off-road vehicle trails as shown on the area map; other graded dirt roads and off-road vehicle trails shown on Forest Service maps and U.S.G.S. topographic quadrangles provide routes for vehicle travel within the National Forest; access into the Dark Canyon Primitive Area is also possible by boat on upper Lake Powell.

AREA NOTES:
1. The non-designated hiking trails, routes and areas listed are just representative samples of the primitive hiking available in this area.
2. The U.S. Forest Service sells two maps of the Abajo Mountains area. One is small, the other much larger. The smaller map is useful only for the alignment of the major roads in the mountains and general vicinity. The larger map is more detailed, but of very limited value to hikers because it does not show surface contours.
3. The foothill canyons in this area are exceptionally rich in archeological sites. Hikers should constantly bear in mind that all such sites and artifacts are protected by state and federal law.

Abajo Mountains

TYPE OF TRAILS: mountain.

TRAIL MILEAGE: optional, unlimited.

TIME TO HIKE: optional, unlimited.

U.S.G.S. MAPS: Monticello, Mt. Linnaeus, Fable Valley, Mouth of Dark Canyon, Natural Bridges, Bears Ears, Brushy Basin Wash and Blanding quadrangles.

HAZARDS: steep slopes; deep canyons; dangerous slopes of loose rubble; dense vegetation in places.

SEASONS: best from late spring through fall, but may be traveled using snowshoes or cross-country skis when snow precludes normal hiking.

ACCESS: access from north is via Utah 211 and road up North Cottonwood Canyon from Dugout Ranch, which becomes Forest Service road #088; access from east is from U.S. 163 via Forest Service road #105 about 4 miles north of Monticello, road #079 from Monticello and #087 just east of Monticello; access from south is from Blanding via Forest Service roads #079 and #24, from Utah 95 via connecting spur to #24, and via other end of #24 near Natural Bridges National Monument; access via Cottonwood Canyon road that branches from #24 is not recommended for highway vehicles.

TRAIL SUMMARY: Although there are quite a few interconnecting, poorly-maintained and marked primitive hiking trails within the Abajo Mountains, most of the hiking there is a combination of following seldom-used or abandoned off-road vehicle trails plus self-guiding through rugged mountain wilderness, with all the usual forest, wildlife, stream, alpine meadows, old log cabins, abandoned mines and similar highlights to be found in all western mountains of similar elevation.

TRAIL HIGHLIGHTS

The National Forest area surrounding the Abajo Mountains can be divided into three sub-areas. The eastern part contains most of the high peaks, the developed campgrounds and most of the established hiking trails and routes. The central part is predominantly wooded highlands that are considerably less attractive to hikers. The western part is cut into a series of wooded highlands and mesas by the upper tributary canyon systems of the Dark Canyon Primitive Area. The roads and trails there are used primarily by hikers for access into various parts of the primitive area. As in the La Sal Mountains, the mountainous eastern part of the Abajos has a poorly-marked and maintained system of hiking trails. The general alignment of these trails is shown on the large Forest Service map of the La Sal and Abajo mountains. Within the same area there are many other worthwhile primitive routes that follow drainage lines, roads and mountain contours between areas and points of interest. Hikers who do not mind following abandoned or seldom-used off-road vehicle trails will find a whole interconnecting network of these in the Abajo Mountains and foothills. One such begins in upper North Cottonwood Canyon near the end of the rough road that penetrates the canyon. Hikers can continue on up the creek drainage line, eventually to connect with other trails and roads, with several branching trails and canyon routes available along the way. Another such route goes up Indian Creek from near Newspaper Rock State Historical Monument on Utah 211. This route also offers branching trails and routes. The big Forest Service map shows still others.

NOTES: The Abajo Mountains are geologically young and hence very steep, with sharply eroded slopes, drainage lines and canyons. Hikers who intend to wilderness hike in these mountains should be well-equipped, experienced and in top physical condition. Potable water is plentiful in the higher elevations of the Abajos, making lengthy backpacking feasible. There is quite often current mining activity in the central part of this area. Hikers would be well-advised to avoid such activities, and to beware of ore trucks on the roads. Hiking in the western part of this area is covered under the Dark Canyon Primitive Area.

Abajo Foothill Canyons

TYPE OF TRAILS: canyon-stream.

TRAIL MILEAGE: optional.

TIME TO HIKE: optional, up to several weeks or more.

U.S.G.S. MAPS: Monticello, Blanding, Brushy Basin Wash and Bears Ears quadrangles.

HAZARDS: very remote area; hazardous drops.

SEASONS: early spring through late fall, or may be hiked winters when snow is light.

ACCESS: access to various foothill canyon systems between Monticello and Natural Bridges National Monument is wherever U.S. 163 or Utah 95 crosses the main or tributary drainage lines; other county or Forest Service roads in the area or National Forest may also be used for access or egress at other points of these canyon systems.

TRAIL SUMMARY: Most of the many canyons crossed by U.S. 163 and Utah 95 between Monticello and Natural Bridges National Monument offer excellent opportunities for exploring the beautiful and virtually unspoiled Abajo foothill canyons that drain to the south, with their wooded, rugged, natural beauty and numerous archeological sites.

TRAIL HIGHLIGHTS

The gentle southern slopes of the Abajo mountain range are cut by a complex series of canyons. The sandstone formations that form these canyons take on endless erosional forms, including waterfalls and potholes, dry and otherwise, echoing amphitheaters and alcoves, sheer or terraced rock walls, dripping spring-seep caves, balanced rocks, arches and natural bridges. The canyons, the terraced slopes above them and the nearby mesa highlands are heavily vegetated. Many of the canyons are rich in fascinating archeological sites. Some canyons are deep. Others are shallower and meandering. Some are dry except for occasional springs or following rain or snow-melt. Others contain intermittent, seasonal or perennial streams. All sooner or later join into one of the few major washes that flow on south to meet the San Juan River, which in turn adds its waters to Lake Powell. Hikers can almost select a wash or canyon at random and find it to be an exciting, and often demanding, hiking route. Some of the major canyons worth exploring upstream from the access highways are Devils Canyon, Recapture Wash, Big Canyon, Brushy Basin Wash, Arch Canyon and their tributaries. Arch Canyon is outstanding, with its steep, terraced walls, arches and several cliff dwellings. All of these drainages, followed upstream, eventually end high in the forested Abajo Mountains or foothill slopes. With careful planning, roads or vehicle trails there can be used for egress, or as routes to the heads of other canyons which can be hiked back toward lower access points. These canyons offer limitless opportunities for backpackers who want to explore higher, cooler canyon country wilderness for several days at a time, because water is relatively plentiful. But whether these canyons are explored as a series of day-hikes from a convenient base camp, or in longer backpack trips, they offer an excellent look at some really wild, remote and beautiful canyon country.

NOTES: Water found in these canyon systems should be purified, except at springs not used by domestic cattle, or from free-flowing streams. Many of the Abajo foothill canyons also offer excellent hiking in the downstream direction. Some of these will be discussed in the San Juan Area section of this book. Most of the land immediately adjacent to the highway between Monticello and the U.S. 163-Utah 95 junction is private land and should be respected, but the two main canyons crossed in this stretch, Devils Canyon and Recapture Creek, are accessible. Others are accessible farther upcanyon from spur roads that go north or west. Virtually all of the land through which Utah 95 travels is publicly owned.

Dark Canyon Primitive Area

TYPE OF TRAILS: canyon-stream.

TRAIL MILEAGE: optional.

TIME TO HIKE: optional, up to several weeks or more.

U.S.G.S. MAPS: Orange Cliffs, The Needles, Fable Valley, Mouth of Dark Canyon, Natural Bridges and Bears Ears quadrangles.

HAZARDS: very remote area; hazardous drops.

SEASONS: early spring through late fall, or may be hiked in winter when snow is light; season is more limited when access is by land.

ACCESS: Access into the Dark Canyon Primitive Area by highway vehicle is limited to times during the late spring, summer and fall when the dirt roads that provide access are free of snow and dry. Access by off-road vehicle is less limited. From Utah 95 there are two approaches: one leaves the highway about 5½ miles west of the U.S. 163-Utah 95 junction; the other leaves the spur road to Natural Bridges National Monument just after it branches from Utah 95. These two approaches are joined together as Forest Service road #24, which gives access to Forest Service road #088 along Elk Ridge. About 1 mile north of the Bears Ears, a road that branches west from #24 goes by the head of Woodenshoe Canyon, an upper tributary of Dark Canyon. At the north end of Elk Ridge, Forest Service road #091 branches west from #088 along North Long Point and then Dark Canyon Plateau. This road gives access to upper Fable Valley and on down Gypsum Canyon, both of which are in the Dark Canyon Primitive Area. Another spur of #088 about 2½ miles north of the #091 turn-off is Forest Service road #093. This road goes north then west into the Beef Basin-Ruins Park Area. The upper end of Gypsum Canyon is accessible from the western end of this loop. To reach Forest Service road #088 from the north, drive west from U.S. 163 on Utah 211; turn south at Dugout Ranch; after 3 miles, turn right across a creek ford, then continue to Cathedral Butte and beyond. This road becomes #088 as it enters the National Forest. The easiest access into the Dark Canyon Primitive Area canyon system is by boat up Lake Powell from Hite, where Utah 95 crosses the lake. The main canyons in the primitive area, Dark, Bowdie and Gypsum, are all accessible by boat when the lake is at its maximum level, although Gypsum may not be accessible some of the time. For current conditions, inquire of rangers at the Hite Marina.

TRAIL SUMMARY: The protected canyon systems within the Dark Canyon Primitive Area are extremely deep, narrow and spectacular in their lower reaches, offering experienced, well-prepared hikers an intimate look at some of the most remote, unspoiled and fascinating gorges in canyon country.

TRAIL HIGHLIGHTS

Dark Canyon Primitive Area is a huge complex of canyons and mesas that has been set aside for protection by the Bureau of Land Management because of its outstanding natural beauty and unspoiled condition. The area's limited accessibility will tend to protect these characteristics, making them a highlight for wilderness-seeking backpackers. Dark Canyon and several of its upper tributaries extend beyond the primitive area boundary into the adjacent National Forest, where the Forest Service has a program for the protection of their unusual scenic and other values. Hikers will find that the best routes into the primitive area by land are by way of Forest Service roads and these upper canyons. The road spur just north of the Bears Ears provides access into Woodenshoe Canyon and on down Dark Canyon below their confluence, Road #88 provides access to upper Dark Canyon by way of Peavine Canyon and Kigalia Canyon. Road #091 provides access to Dark Canyon via Trail Canyon, and to Gypsum Canyon via Fable Valley. These access points along the Forest Service and BLM road system in the area permit loop hikes along the upper primitive area canyons. One such loop goes down Woodenshoe to Dark Canyon, up Dark Canyon, then out by way of Trail Canyon. Another loop goes down Fable Valley, then out by way of upper Gypsum Canyon to the Beef Basin road. These loops can be hiked either direction and can be supplemented by treks on down Dark or Gypsum. Although Dark Canyon Plateau is not included within the primitive area, the road that travels this high, branching peninsula between the Dark and Bowdie canyon systems can be used for access to Bowdie Canyon. Those who plan to explore the primitive area from boat access on Lake Powell should be prepared to boat for a distance up the lake from Hite and a short distance into the lower canyons. From where the water ends in the lower canyons, it is sometimes necessary to negotiate on foot a stretch of wash that the fluctuating lake level has disturbed. No matter how access to this vast canyon system is gained, however, hikers will find it to be one of the most outstanding in every respect in the entire canyon country region.

NOTES: As with other Abajo foothill canyons, the various major and tributary canyons within and leading into the Dark Canyon Primitive Area have streams that are seasonal or intermittent. There should be adequate water, however, for extended backpacking, and most of the water sources will be potable without treatment, although some are highly mineralized. Hiking within these remote and rugged canyons should be attempted only by experienced hikers who are well-prepared and in good physical condition. Those seeking access via the noted dirt roads should constantly watch for road hazards. The use of an off-road vehicle for land access is highly recommended. Hikers with an interest in prehistoric ruins will find it very worthwhile to explore the Ruins Park area, where a number of Anasazi stone structures are scattered around over several square miles.

Natural Bridges National Monument

TYPE OF TRAILS: designated.

TRAIL MILEAGE: optional, up to 9 miles or more.

TIME TO HIKE: optional, up to 1 day or more.

U.S.G.S. MAPS: Natural Bridges and Bears Ears quadrangles.

HAZARDS: hazardous drops.

SEASONS: best during cooler months of spring or fall, but may be hiked in summer, or winter when snow is light.

ACCESS: drive west on Utah 95 from U.S. 163; about 2 miles west of the Utah 95-Utah 261 junction, turn right on paved road to Natural Bridges National Monument; within monument, drive on beyond visitor center around road loop to pull-outs near each of the three largest natural bridges in the monument; foot trails start at pull-outs nearest each bridge.

TRAIL SUMMARY: The hiking trails that go to and between the three major natural spans in Natural Bridges National Monument provide breathtaking views of these very large and beautiful natural bridges, the lovely wilderness canyons they span and a number of archaeological sites.

TRAIL HIGHLIGHTS

There are short foot trails to each of the three major spans within Natural Bridges National Monument. Each begins at pull-outs along the loop road that travels counter-clockwise around the perimeter of the narrow-necked peninsula that is formed by White and Armstrong canyons within the monument. The first trailhead reached goes to Sipapu Natural Bridge. This trail descends steeply into picturesque White Canyon via steps, ledges and ladders, past archeological sites and breathtaking viewpoints overlooking the canyon and bridge. The trail is only 1¼ miles round trip, but is very steep all the way. The trail down to Kachina Natural Bridge is about 1½ miles round trip and similar to the Sipapu trail. The trail to Owachomo Natural Bridge is only ½ mile round trip and the grade is much more gradual. All three of these huge and beautiful bridges can be seen from pull-outs along the canyon-rim road, but their sheer size, bulk and beauty can only be appreciated from directly below. For hikers who want the best possible look at these bridges, the lovely, watered canyons they span and the many other natural erosional features in between, the best approach is to take a full day's hike along the canyons between the three bridges. One way to do this is to park at the Sipapu trailhead, go down to Sipapu, then down White Canyon to Kachina at the confluence of White and Armstrong canyons, up Armstrong to Owachomo, up to the loop road, then on across the wooded peninsula on the designated trail that connects with the Sipapu trailhead pull-out. This complete loop is 9 miles long, but can be shortened to 7 by having a vehicle at the Owachomo pull-out. The hike along these canyons is lovely in any season, with their intermittent streams, pools, trees, wildflowers, arches, balanced rocks, sheer cliffs and cliff-dwellings, but especially so in the autumn when the cottonwoods are golden. There are many annual and some perennial wildflowers in the spring. Other perennials and shrubs bloom in the fall, making the canyons vividly colorful most of the warmer season.

NOTES: Hikers with the time will find it rewarding to hike on up the branching canyons above Sipapu and Owachomo natural bridges. The canyon-bottom trail between the three big bridges is a designated route, but not a well-defined trail. It follows the wash-bottom most of the way, detouring onto higher ground only when forced to by water, dense vegetation or rock ledges. Although there is water in the canyons in the monument, especially in the spring and early summer, hikers should carry their own water for one-day hikes. Good water is available at the visitor center in the monument. The Park Service issues a small hiking trail map of the monument. This is also available at the visitor center. The relative ages of the three great natural bridges are: Kachina, quite young, with its opening still growing; Sipapu mature, with its opening stable; Owachomo quite old, and slowly thinning toward its eventual collapse.

White Canyon

TYPE OF TRAIL: canyon-stream.

TRAIL MILEAGE: optional, up to 40 miles or more.

TIME TO HIKE: optional, up to 2 weeks or more.

U.S.G.S. MAPS: Bears Ears, Natural Bridges, Mancos Mesa, Browns Rim and Mouth of Dark Canyon quadrangles.

HAZARDS: hazardous drops; flash-flooding.

SEASONS: early spring through late fall, and winter when snow is light.

ACCESS: for access near upper end of canyon, drive into Natural Bridges National Monument and hike down into White Canyon at either Sipapu or Kachina natural bridges; for access via Armstrong Canyon, hike down to Owachomo Natural Bridge, go down canyon to the confluence with White Canyon; for other access or egress points, drive toward the Hite area of Lake Powell on Utah 95; there are many places to the east of the highway where White Canyon is easily accessible; for access or egress at lower end of canyon, enter or leave just upstream of Utah 95 White Canyon bridge.

TRAIL SUMMARY: White Canyon is a very long, winding, picturesque canyon of intermediate depth with an intermittent, seasonal stream, white sandstone walls, water-loving vegetation and several long side-canyons worth exploring.

TRAIL HIGHLIGHTS

White Canyon drains a large segment of the Abajo Mountains and their southwestern foothills. The main canyon is more than 40 miles long and has numerous tributary canyons, some of them also quite long. White Canyon begins just east of Natural Bridges National Monument, winds through the wooded monument as a deep, white-rimmed gorge and is joined near the monument's western boundary by the Armstrong Canyon system. It then heads northwestward through beautifully colorful redrock country with its white rimlands expanding for many miles to create a great maze of bright slickrock set within higher terraces and slopes of dark red Moenkopi and Chinle sediments. Toward its lower end, the canyon deepens and narrows to form a twisting slash near the shores of Lake Powell. The canyon in the vicinity of the Utah 95 bridge is virtually impassable, forcing all but the most determined hikers to leave the canyon before its end. The long, meandering canyon can be entered many places, within Natural Bridges National Monument and on down-canyon. Utah 95 roughly parallels the main canyon to the west, providing many opportunities to enter or leave the canyon via several off-road vehicle trails, or by climbing the canyon walls. This is easy in many places, thus allowing hikers to explore the lovely canyon system in segments, from nearby base camps. Along the canyon floor, hikers will see many things of interest. Major tributaries offer convenient access into higher Abajo foothills areas. Two of these especially worth exploring are Gravel and Cheesebox canyons. The intermittent stream in White Canyon has countless pools, and supports a wide variety of plant and animal life. The layered Cedar Mesa sandstone canyon walls have eroded into countless fascinating shapes and forms, and alert hikers will discover archeological sites along these walls in sheltered alcoves and undercut ledges. The only traces of modern man in the canyon are near the few places where off-road vehicle trails leave Utah 95 to cross the canyon and enter the wilderness country to the east. Such minor trespasses on this long and lovely wilderness canyon are soon forgotten as the next bend is rounded and some fascinating natural wonder appears, or another mysterious side-canyon beckons.

NOTES: Water found in White Canyon and its tributaries should be purified before drinking, except at springs not used by domestic cattle.

Ghouls

The canyon rim we were following was delightful.

The rimlands were almost solid Kayenta sandstone, creating a continuing series of weathered terraces, tiny caves, undercut ledges and great, broken slabs tilted crazily from being undermined by rain-and-wind erosion beyond their endurance. Every few yards an ornate, natural rock-garden set with gnarled junipers and brilliantly colored desert wildflowers and blooming shrubs greeted us with wild compositions and dazzling spring beauty.

Below the rim, a narrow, sheer-walled gorge twisted and turned like a great, sinuous serpent, its bottom now open and set with reflective pools of water along the flowing stream, now choked with gigantic, angular boulders half the size of houses. Feathery, blossoming fronds of tamarisk lined the watercourse in many places, sharing the precious desert moisture with other less conspicuous forms of life. On down the gorge, we could barely see what might be a huge arch in the opposite cliff.

But what held my attention for the moment was well back from this enchanting rim, where still higher walls and domes of rounded, convoluted Navajo sandstone terminated the broad canyon-rim terrace we were following. There, perhaps a quarter mile away and beyond a rising, wooded slope of dune sand, I could see a big spring-seep alcove almost entirely hidden from casual gaze by taller trees and heavier brush. The vegetation in the shallow gully below the alcove was richer, thicker, taller than usual.

Water—at least a small seasonal flow, maybe even a perennial trickle. And where there was a reliable source of water and a big, well-hidden cave, there might also be other interesting things—like Anasazi Indian ruins!

I had learned long ago to follow my hunches while exploring the wild and remote canyon country of southeastern Utah, occasionally to no avail, but more often to some exciting and unexpected highlight of natural or human origin.

148

As we hiked across the level ground and entered the shallow, overgrown gully that led up to the big cave, we encountered flowing water—not much, just a trickle, but a surface trickle in such terrain means considerably more beneath the surface.

Our route steepened, then left the brush and trees to ascend a dusty, rocky slope overhung by the cave's water-streaked ceiling.

And there! My hunch had really paid off! There were the remains of several ancient rock-and-mud dwellings, mostly buried in dust the desert winds had dumped in the big alcove over the centuries. On the top of one huge boulder, a small rock granary was largely intact, but the other structures were in poor condition.

No matter—this had to be a dwelling site of the prehistoric Anasazi culture! The Fremonts had not settled this side of the Colorado River gorge. Yet I knew of no other Anasazi settlements this far north. Hunting camps, chipping grounds, petroglyph and pictograph panels, isolated granaries—yes. But no other dwellings, making this find exceptionally valuable—the extreme outpost of an entire culture.

Unfortunately, we had not been the first to find the dwellings, although we were the first to report it to the appropriate authorities. Those who had been there before us were not likely to have told anyone else, let alone the appropriate federal officials, or scientists at one of Utah's universities, because they were the lowest kind of vandals—they were ghouls, grave-robbers!

Two big pits, dug into the roofless remnants of these ancient and valuable prehistoric dwellings, gave ample evidence of the nature of those who had been here earlier. Buried stone walls were damaged or destroyed by the type of mindless digging that makes archeologists shudder, and dozens of human bones lay about in random disarray, carelessly thrown aside in the search for collectible, saleable artifacts, with complete, almost disdainful disregard for the federal and state laws protecting such sites, and for the scientific values that were being destroyed forever.

For long minutes we stared down at this scene of vandalism, a scene all too familiar in the remote reaches of canyon country, comparing in our minds the probable value of the miserable few artifacts that might have been found, with the irreversible loss of scientific and cultural data. How tragic! How short-sighted! How greedy these vandals had been!

Then it struck me—all those human bones, some child-sized! Enough to be the mortal remains of several people—but no skulls! These were not ordinary vandals of the pot-and-point-hunter variety, these were ghouls, digging into ancient graves for possible artifacts, yes, but also for the skulls of a people not only dead as individuals, but extinct as an entire prehistoric culture!

As we sadly left the cave, our thrill of discovery dampened by our personal encounter with the work of modern vandals and ghouls, we wondered whose fireplace mantel, whose living room coffee table, was now decorated with a grotesque row of grinning skulls, the pitiful remains of a group, perhaps a whole family, of original Americans.

And for what civilized purpose?

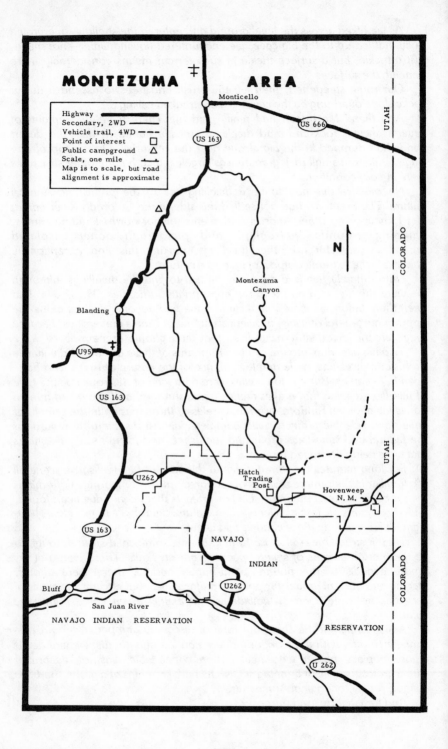

MONTEZUMA AREA

Highway
Secondary, 2WD
Vehicle trail, 4WD
Point of interest ☐
Public campground △
Scale, one mile
Map is to scale, but road
alignment is approximate

Monticello

US 666

UTAH

US 163

Montezuma
Canyon

N

COLORADO

Blanding

U95

US 163

U262

Hatch
Trading
Post

Hovenweep
N. M.

UTAH

US 163

NAVAJO

INDIAN

Bluff

U262

San Juan River

NAVAJO INDIAN RESERVATION

RESERVATION

COLORADO

U 262

Montezuma Area

AREA NAME: this area was named after Montezuma Canyon, the long, branching gorge that drains most of the area.

AREA BOUNDARIES: U.S. 163, U.S. 666, the Colorado-Utah border and the northern boundary of the Navajo Indian Reservation.

U.S.G.S. TOPOGRAPHIC MAPS THAT COVER THE AREA: Monticello, Eastland, Monument Canyon, Blanding, Bluff, Montezuma Creek and Cajon Mesa quadrangles.

GENERAL TOPOGRAPHY: elevated, wooded highlands slashed deeply by two major drainage systems, Montezuma Creek and Recapture Creek, and their many tributaries.

SUGGESTED BASE CAMPS: motels or commercial campgrounds in Monticello, Blanding and Bluff; developed public campgrounds at Hovenweep National Monument, at Sand Island west of Bluff, and at Devils Canyon near U.S. 163; primitive camping is permitted almost anywhere in the area except on private land, which is generally posted, or within Hovenweep National Monument; contact park rangers for current regulations there.

ACCESS ROUTES: U.S. 163, U.S. 666, Utah 262, county roads and off-road vehicle trails as shown on the area map.

AREA NOTES:
1.   The non-designated hiking trails, routes and areas listed are just representative samples of the primitive hiking available in this area.
2.   The relatively level highlands in the northern part of this area are largely private property and under cultivation, as are some areas to the east of U.S. 163.
3.   Before leaving public highways and roads that penetrate the Navajo Indian Reservation, hikers should make local inquiry. The Navajo Nation has its own system of regulations which are sometimes vigorously enforced by their own police.
4.   This area is exceptionally rich in archeological sites. Hikers should constantly bear in mind that all such sites and artifacts are protected by state and federal law.

Hovenweep

TYPE OF TRAIL: designated.

TRAIL MILEAGE: optional, up to 2 miles or more.

TIME TO HIKE: optional, up to 1 day or more.

U.S.G.S. MAPS: Cajon Mesa quadrangle.

HAZARDS: hazardous drops.

SEASONS: best during cooler months of spring or fall, but may be hiked in summer, or winter when snow is light.

ACCESS: drive east from U.S. 163 on Utah 262; after about 8½ miles, leave Utah 262 and continue eastward, following road signs to Hatch Trading Post and on to Hovenweep National Monument; park at visitor center; trail starts here.

TRAIL SUMMARY: This short canyon and canyon-rim trail provides a close look at a series of beautifully preserved Anasazi cliff dwellings, related archeological sites and the watered canyon that once supported this fair-sized settlement of prehistoric Indians.

TRAIL HIGHLIGHTS

This easy trail and its several short spurs can be traveled all or in part, depending upon time available and interest in such remnants of a now-extinct stone-age culture. A trail guide provided by the Park Service gives details about that culture, the fascinating ruins along and below the canyon rim and some of the natural history of such canyons in the open desert. Multi-storied, roofless dwellings made of stone and mud stand along the shallow canyon rim. Sturdy rock towers balance on top of huge boulders just below the rim. Overhanging ledges are still partly walled in and rubbly slopes below the rim bear mute testimony to stone dwellings built on foundations less stable than solid rock. On one wall, petroglyphs depict an odd-shaped bird, and in the canyon's upper end a big cavern with dripping walls is almost hidden behind masses of trees and shrubs. Those who wish to see more such Anasazi ruins can hike on down the canyon rim toward the campground, or visit other isolated sites scattered throughout the region with names such as Cajon, Holly, Hackberry, Cutthroat Castle and Goodman Point. The last four of these sites are just across the border in Colorado.

NOTES: Hovenweep National Monument includes several scattered ruins sites. All such sites are protected by federal law. Park rangers are usually willing to give directions to other Hovenweep sites for those who have a serious interest in early American Indian cultures. The spur roads to some of these sites are marginal at best for highway vehicles, but are generally short enough to hike. Another ruins site worth visiting is just over the border in Colorado.

Montezuma Canyon

TYPE OF TRAIL: canyon-stream.

TRAIL MILEAGE: optional.

TIME TO HIKE: optional, up to several weeks or more.

U.S.G.S. MAPS: Monticello, Eastland, Monument Canyon, Blanding, Montezuma Creek and Cajon Mesa quadrangles.

HAZARDS: limited water in tributary canyons; remote location; hazardous drops.

SEASONS: best during cooler months of spring or fall, but may be hiked in summer, or winter when snow is light.

ACCESS: for access near upper end of canyon, drive south from Monticello on U.S. 163 for 5 miles; turn east on gravelled road, which drops into canyon in about another 5 miles; for access near lower end of canyon, drive east from U.S. 163 on Utah 262 and follow signs eastward to Hatch Trading Post; road upcanyon begins here; other graded dirt roads and off-road vehicle trails enter the canyon system from both sides between these main approaches.

TRAIL SUMMARY: Enormous, branching Montezuma Canyon offers limitless opportunities for exploring fascinating canyon country wilderness that is rich in natural beauty, historic and prehistoric sites, and also affords good rockhounding, all within convenient range of a rough but passable backcountry road.

TRAIL HIGHLIGHTS

Montezuma Creek originates high in the Abajo Mountains southwest of Monticello. After leaving the National Forest and crossing several miles of cultivated farmlands, the intermittent, seasonal creek turns south and plunges abruptly into a deep and lovely canyon. The upper access road drops into the canyon about 5 miles below this point. The undeveloped stretch upcanyon from this access point is worth exploring. For the next 35 miles, Montezuma Canyon winds and twists between picturesque slickrock walls topped with layered deposits that are fairly heavily wooded. Along the way, the slickrock walls gradually disappear, as the geologic strata slope downward toward the south. The canyon floor slowly widens, but is relatively flat, heavily vegetated and under cultivation in some of its broader stretches. The meandering stream course cuts deeply into the canyon bottom sediments and is bordered by cottonwoods and other trees. The road down the canyon is rough but serviceable for highway vehicles for most of the distance to Hatch Trading Post, but is marginal in some places. The road fords creek lines several times, which could cause problems during periods of heavy water flow. Even though part of the canyon floor is under cultivation, and there are occasional ranch struc-

tures near the road, it is worth hiking many long stretches of the creek that are not near the road, and most of the many side-canyons are unspoiled and well worth exploring. In some long stretches, it is worth the effort to hike along the base of the eastern wall of the canyon, where some of the many natural caves there contain the ruins of Anasazi Indian structures. At one point, there is a large group of cliff-dwellings in the western wall, and in one rather primitive part of the lower canyon, a valley-floor ruin near the road has been partially restored by archeologists. A completely restored kiva can be entered via its roof-hole. Many of the side-canyons contain archeological sites that can only be reached by hiking. Some of the larger side-canyons are penetrated for a short distance by off-road vehicle trails that were built to support mineral search activities. A few of these trails continue on out of the canyon system into the wooded highlands. One long tributary of Montezuma Canyon called Devils Canyon crosses U.S. 163 midway between Monticello and Blanding. Hiking the picturesque 15 mile stretch of Devils Canyon between U.S. 163 and Montezuma Canyon makes an excellent two-day jaunt. Near Hatch Trading Post, the canyon enters one arm of the Navajo Indian Reservation. Below the trading post, the creek line is a patchwork of private and reservation land on to its confluence with the San Juan River. This stretch offers little to hikers, but there is more than enough excellent hiking in Montezuma Canyon and its tributaries north of Hatch Trading Post to afford weeks, or even months, of backpack exploring or day-hiking from base camps.

NOTES: The water flow in Montezuma Creek is variable with the seasons, and is diverted for agriculture in some places, but there is almost always water available at various places within the main canyon and its major branches. Such water should be purified, except at springs that are not used by domestic livestock. Some of the ranch structures in Montezuma Canyon are old enough to be of historic significance, and some of the old farm implements make excellent photographic subjects. Although most of the private land in the canyon is fenced but not posted, hikers should respect such property. Some of the side roads have gates. Unless posted otherwise, such gates are for cattle control, and may be used for access into undeveloped areas. Hikers should avoid any areas posted because of current mining activity.

Recapture Creek

TYPE OF TRAIL: canyon-stream.

TRAIL MILEAGE: optional.

TIME TO HIKE: optional, up to several weeks or more.

U.S.G.S. MAPS: Blanding, Montezuma Creek and Bluff quadrangles.

HAZARDS: water sources seasonal and scattered; remote location, hazardous drops.

SEASONS: best during cooler months of spring or fall, but may be hiked in summer, or winter when snow is light.

ACCESS: drive east from U.S. 163 on any road or off-road vehicle trail between Blanding and Bluff; most of these will cross Recapture Creek or one of its many tributary canyons; U.S. 163 crosses Recapture Creek about 4½ miles north of Blanding.

TRAIL SUMMARY: Hiking the main canyon of Recapture Creek and its several long tributaries provides a look at historic and prehistoric sites and a lot of very wild canyon country that is seldom viewed by anyone.

TRAIL HIGHLIGHTS

Recapture Creek originates high in the Abajo Mountains north of Blanding. A few miles after leaving the National Forest, this seasonal, intermittent stream goes east under U.S. 163 in a broad, deep valley, then heads south and roughly parallel with the highway but several miles east, to its confluence with the San Juan River 5 miles east of Bluff. The long stretch of canyon between U.S. 163 and Utah 262 provides the best and wettest hiking within this area. South of Utah

262, the wash continues for about 3 miles between separating canyon walls and is paralleled by an off-road vehicle trail. From there on to the San Juan River, Recapture Creek is largely a broad, open desert wash with sparse vegetation and few signs of water except during major run-off periods. Hikers will find that the long, primitive stretch of Recapture Creek north of U.S. 163 and on to its origin provides a demanding but rewarding mountain wilderness experience, but the best canyon-stream hiking is the 18 to 20 miles between U.S. 163 and Utah 262. For those who want a shorter hike, a gravelled road crosses the main canyon about midway. This road goes to U.S. 163 or Blanding to the west, or on to Montezuma Canyon to the east. Along the length of Recapture Creek, several major branching canyons offer still more opportunities to explore this colorful desert-canyon wilderness. There are many archeological sites within the canyon system. A very nice one can be seen in one tributary, Brown Canyon, near where a county road crosses the wash. Although some of the highlands to the west of the main canyon have been developed for agriculture, except for a very few places at or near where roads or vehicle trails cross or parallel the wash for a short distance, the many miles of the Recapture canyon system are wild and unspoiled, making them ideal for back-packers or day-hikers who want to explore some very interesting and empty canyon backcountry.

NOTES: water found in this canyon system should be purified, except at springs not used by domestic cattle. The water is usually highly mineralized. The geologic strata through which Recapture Creek flows south of U.S. 163 offer good rockhounding.

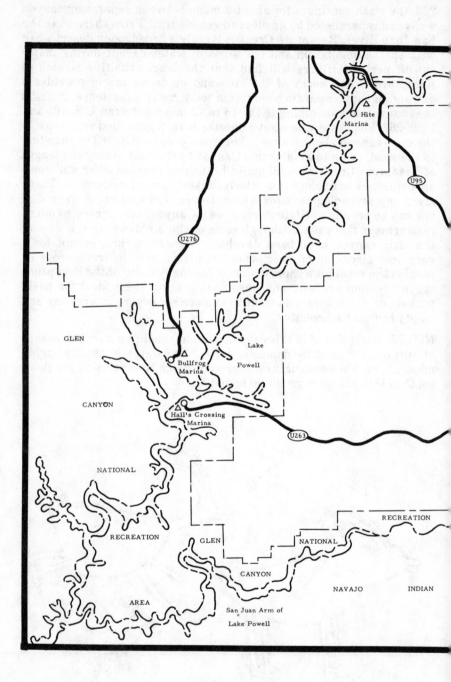

San Juan Area

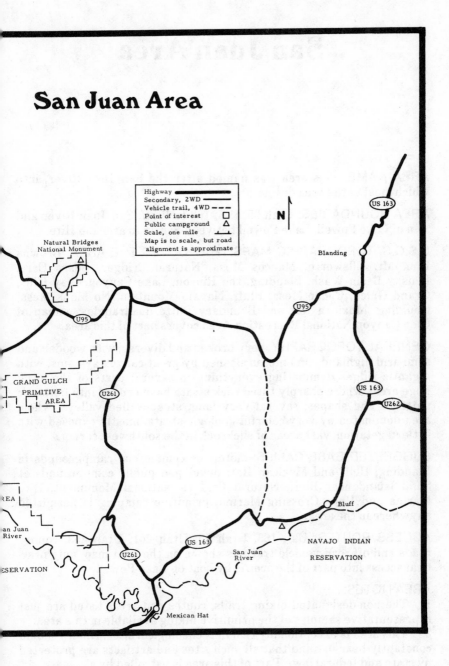

Highway
Secondary, 2WD
Vehicle trail, 4WD
Point of interest □
Public campground △
Scale, one mile
Map is to scale, but road alignment is approximate

N

Natural Bridges
National Monument

US 163

Blanding

U95

U95

GRAND GULCH
PRIMITIVE
AREA

U261

US 163

U262

Bluff

AREA

an Juan
River

US 163

NAVAJO INDIAN

U261

San Juan
River

RESERVATION

ESERVATION

Mexican Hat

San Juan Area

AREA NAME: This area was named after the San Juan River, into which most of the area drains.

AREA BOUNDARIES: Utah 95, U.S. 163 to Bluff, San Juan River and arm of Lake Powell, Lake Powell between San Juan arm and Hite.

U.S.G.S. TOPOGRAPHIC MAPS THAT COVER THE AREA: Browns Rim, Mt. Ellsworth, Mancos Mesa, Natural Bridges, Bears Ears, Brushy Basin Wash, Blanding, the Rincon, Lake Canyon, Clay Hills, Grand Gulch, Cedar Mesa, Bluff, Navajo Mountain, No Mans Mesa, Goulding, Mexican Hat and Boundary Butte quadrangles; a map of Glen Canyon National Recreation Area covers part of this area.

GENERAL TOPOGRAPHY: very broken and diverse, with wooded and semi-arid highlands and mesas slashed by great canyon systems, with gigantic ridges dominating everything in several parts of the area; huge areas where sharply tilted rock strata have eroded into fantastic patterns and shapes; several very long, steep-walled valleys; whole area dominated by very colorful geologic strata, mostly exposed with little vegetation; vast areas of slickrock in the southwest corner.

SUGGESTED BASE CAMPS: motels or commercial campgrounds in Blanding, Bluff and Mexican Hat; developed public campgrounds at Sand Island near Bluff, Natural Bridges National Monument, Hite Marina and Halls Crossing Marina; primitive camping is permitted anywhere in the area.

ACCESS ROUTES: U.S. 163, Utah 95, Utah 261, Utah 263, county roads and off-road vehicle trails as shown on the area map; only practical access into part of the area is by boat on Lake Powell.

AREA NOTES:
1. The non-designated hiking trails, routes and areas listed are just representative samples of the primitive hiking available in this area.
2. This area is exceptionally rich in archeological sites. Hikers should constantly bear in mind that all such sites and artifacts are protected by state and federal laws. Part of this area is patrolled by air.
3. This huge desert-canyon wilderness area is very lightly traveled

except on the few paved roads, is unpopulated except at perimeter settlements at Bluff, Mexican Hat, Natural Bridges National Monument and the two Lake Powell marinas at Hite and Halls Crossing, and is far from any major sources of supplies or services, including medical aid. Those planning extensive hikes into this remote canyon country should plan accordingly.

Comb Ridge

TYPE OF TRAIL: slickrock.

TRAIL MILEAGE: optional; 20 miles along suggested route.

TIME TO HIKE: optional; 3 to 4 days along suggested route.

U.S.G.S. MAPS: Brushy Basin Wash, Bluff and Boundary Butte quadrangles.

HAZARDS: limited water; hazardous cliffs; remote location; very hot in summer.

SEASONS: best during cooler months of spring or fall, or winter when snow is light; not recommended June through August.

ACCESS: for access near northern end of ridge, drive west on Utah 95 from U.S. 163; Utah 95 cuts through Comb Ridge about 10 miles west of U.S. 163; for access or egress farther south, U.S. 163 goes through a discontinuity in Comb Ridge about 7 miles west of Bluff.

TRAIL SUMMARY: Hiking the elevated, rocky spine of Comb Ridge offers rare highlights in slickrock wilderness, desert-canyon panoramic beauty and sandstone erosional forms along its entire length, plus archeological sites along its southern stretches.

TRAIL HIGHLIGHTS

Comb Ridge is a long "hogback" of ancient sandstone that originates in the foothills of the Abajo Mountains west of Blanding, heads south to intersect U.S. 163 west of Bluff, continues on south through Monument Valley and on into Arizona. Along the way, the ridge is discontinuous in places, such as in the Monument Valley area, and is cut by eons of erosion in many other places. Its northernmost stretch, however, is some 28 miles of fairly continuous Navajo sandstone. This stretch affords hikers a challenging route through desert-canyon wilderness that is rarely seen by anyone. One convenient length of ridge lies between Utah 95 west of Blanding, and U.S. 163 west of Bluff. This route is some 20 miles long, with only a few rarely traveled and remote off-road vehicle trails for egress between the highways. Comb Ridge can also be hiked north from Utah 95 for 5 miles as a slickrock spine before it is absorbed by the Abajo foothills and deeply cut by foothill canyons. Hiking all or part of this stretch from Utah 95 can provide a one-day sample of what Comb Ridge has to offer. The present alignment of Utah 95 goes through a deep cut blasted through the solid sandstone spine of Comb Ridge about 2 miles south of where the old alignment angled down a steep draw. Along the ridge south from Utah 95, the scenery is quite different on the east and west sides of the elevated "hogback." To the east are rolling highlands cut with minor canyons that drain into Butler Wash at the base of the slickrock slope. Pinyon-juniper forest approaches the ridge, to break like dark green ocean waves on the solid rock base. Bright green lines of cottonwoods and other deciduous trees snake along Butler Wash and its watered tributaries. To the west, the ridge falls away in sheer cliffs and mighty talus slopes into the broad bottomland of Comb Wash, where still more verdant lines of water-loving trees mark the meandering main wash and converging drainage lines from the multitude of tributary canyons that cut into the higher country farther west. About midway between Utah 95 and U.S. 163, the highland vegetation becomes more sparse, Butler Wash grows in size and arid desert-land slowly dominates the distant panoramas. There are many Indian ruins along the eastern slopes of Comb Ridge in the central miles of this route. The locations of a few are shown on the Bluff topographic quadrangle. Here, too, a long canyon system that enters Comb Wash from the northwest is rich in archeological sites, although getting down from the ridge to explore them presents a problem. Along the last miles of this route, the ridge is slashed by numerous small gorges and drainage lines, making progress difficult in places, and the surrounding country becomes outrageously eroded and colorful desert, with the sparse vegetation typical of such regions. Comb Ridge continues on south of U.S. 163 for 3 miles before reaching the San Juan River. An interesting 8-mile loop route here goes south on Comb Ridge to the river, upriver to Butler Wash, then back up this wash to U.S. 163. There are still other Indian ruins along the river cliffs and in this stretch of Butler Wash.

NOTES: Hiking Comb Ridge is strenuous and demanding in places. While water can be found in a few places along Butler Wash, the only water available along the top of Comb Ridge would be in potholes following rain. Comb Ridge south of the San Juan River is in the Navajo Indian reservation.

Fish Creek

TYPE OF TRAIL: canyon-stream.

TRAIL MILEAGE: optional, up to 35 miles or more.

TIME TO HIKE: optional, up to 6 days or more.

U.S.G.S. MAPS: Bluff, Cedar Mesa and Bears Ears quadrangles.

HAZARDS: limited, seasonal water; remote area; hazardous drops.

SEASONS: best during cooler months of spring or fall, or winters when snow is light; not recommended mid-June through mid-August.

ACCESS: for access at upper end of canyon system, drive west on Utah 95 from U.S. 163; about 11 miles west of Comb Wash, hike down upper Fish Creek drainage line; one access into upper Owl Creek tributary drainage is via an off-road vehicle trail that goes east from Utah 261 about 6 miles south of Utah 95; for access or egress at lower end of canyon system, drive south on off-road vehicle trail in Comb Wash; Fish Creek canyon enters Comb Wash about 11 miles south of Utah 95.

TRAIL SUMMARY: Deep and lovely Fish Creek canyon and its major tributary, Owl Creek canyon, offer hikers a close look at a beautiful canyon system, several big arches and many Indian ruins rarely seen by anyone.

TRAIL HIGHLIGHTS

The Fish Creek-Owl Creek canyon complex is long and picturesque as it cuts deeply into the wooded Abajo foothills eventually to join Comb Wash. Both the main and south fork of the Fish Creek drainage lines cut deeply into Cedar Mesa sandstone just south of Utah 95. These intermittent, seasonal creeks supported numerous Anasazi settlements. The ruins of these begin about 6 miles down-canyon from Utah 95 and are then frequent all the way to Comb Wash. Owl Creek canyon, a major tributary of Fish Creek, also has many ruins, even in its branching upper end. Off-road vehicle trails provide convenient access or egress from the upper branches of Owl Creek. A 24 mile loop route goes down Fish Creek from Utah 95 to the Owl Creek confluence, then up Owl Creek to an off-road vehicle trail that travels 2 miles west to Utah 261. Hikers with the time and stamina will find it very worthwhile to see the entire canyon system. It takes a minimum of 4 days to go down Fish Creek from Utah 95 to Comb Wash, then back up again and on out to Utah 261 via Owl Creek. If time is spent visiting the many ruins in the main and spur canyons, plan on at least 6 or 7 days. Exploring all the side-canyons will still further extend this time, but will provide many other natural and prehistoric highlights.

NOTES: The vehicle trail down Comb Wash will not be passable

during periods of heavy runoff, because the trail crosses the wash bottom in several places. The Bluff and Cedar Mesa topographic quadrangles show the locations of a number of arches and ruins on the Fish Creek-Owl Creek canyon system. Hikers are reminded that all archeological sites and artifacts are protected by federal and state law.

Grand Gulch Primitive Area

TYPE OF TRAIL: designated.

TRAIL MILEAGE: optional, 7 to 100 miles or more, round trip.

TIME TO HIKE: optional, 1 to 14 days or more.

U.S.G.S. MAPS: Bears Ears, Cedar Mesa and Grand Gulch quadrangles.

HAZARDS: limited, seasonal water; hazardous drops; remote location.

SEASONS: best during cooler months of spring or fall, but may be hiked in summer, or winter when snow is light.

ACCESS: drive west on Utah 95 from U.S. 163; turn south on Utah 261; main access to Grand Gulch Primitive Area is about 3 miles south of Utah 95-Utah 261 junction; another access or egress point is via an off-road vehicle trail that leaves Utah 263 about 7 miles from the Utah 95-Utah 263 junction; access is via Collins Spring, about 6 miles from Utah 263; another access or egress point is via upper Bullet Canyon drainage, which crosses Utah 261 about 11 miles south of Utah 95; access to lower end of Grand Gulch is possible via an off-road vehicle trail that leaves Utah 261 about 12 miles south of Utah 95, then down Slickhorn Canyon and the San Juan River gorge.

TRAIL SUMMARY: The Grand Gulch Primitive Area offers backpackers endless opportunities to explore a long, deep and spectacular canyon system that is rich in natural beauty and archeological sites.

TRAIL HIGHLIGHTS

Grand Gulch is considered by many to be the ultimate in canyon-stream backpacking. Between the upper end of this long, meandering canyon and its confluence with the San Juan River it is about 25 air-miles, but as hikers follow the tortuously twisting canyon bottom, the distance is more like 45 miles. The trail that drops into the upper part of this typical canyon country sandstone gorge is so steep and rugged that it takes a full day just to enter the canyon, go to the nearest ruins about 3½ miles down the trail, then back out. It is thus necessary to backpack if much of this spectacular wilderness canyon is to be seen. A popular three-day hike goes down Grand Gulch to the mouth of Bullet Canyon, then up this canyon to Utah 261. This provides a little better sample of the prehistoric values and natural beauty in this primitive area, but still leaves many miles of the main gorge untouched. To really see this wondrous canyon and all it has to offer takes 10 to 15 days, depending upon how much time is spent seeking out and studying the many ruins and other archeological sites along the way, and how much time is spent at campsites savoring the timeless mood and breathtaking beauty of this unspoiled desert gorge. An ideal route for such a leisurely jaunt would be down Grand Gulch, up each major side-canyon to the archeological sites there, on down to the San Juan River, up the river bank to Slickhorn Canyon, up this canyon to its end, then out to Utah 261 via the off-road vehicle trail. The major side-canyons to Grand Gulch that are worth investigating are Step Canyon and Bullet Canyon, but several other unnamed spur canyons also contain archeological sites or natural highlights worth seeing. In addition to the more obvious ruins sites, there are many inconspicuous panels of Anasazi rock art worth finding. Although a few ruins, arches and other features are located on the Bears Ears, Cedar Mesa and Grand Gulch topographic quadrangles, there are many more. There are no maps available to the public that show all the archeological sites in Grand Gulch and its tributary canyons, but part of exploring this remote canyon system is the challenge and excitement of finding such sites.

There are also ruins in Slickhorn Canyon, especially in its three upper arms.

NOTES: The Grand Gulch Primitive Area was established by the Bureau of Land Management, and is managed and patrolled by BLM rangers. Contact BLM rangers for a summary of regulations governing the use of Grand Gulch. These rangers are knowledgeable about the canyon's many highlights and are always willing to be helpful. Hikers should always register with rangers at the main access point near Utah 261 before entering the gorge from any point. A BLM map of the primitive area available at its main access point shows sources of water in the main canyon and its tributaries. Some water may be highly mineralized, but most canyon sources are potable with little or no treatment because the canyon is closed to domestic grazing. Inquire of the BLM concerning outfitters authorized to enter Grand Gulch with saddle and pack horses. Some hikers may find it worthwhile to use such horses on longer trips down the canyon. Grand Gulch is exceptionally rich in archeological sites. Hikers should bear in mind that all such sites and artifacts are protected by federal law. Grand Gulch is regularly patrolled by land and air.

Johns Canyon Rim

TYPE OF TRAIL: canyon-rim.

TRAIL MILEAGE: optional, up to 35 miles or more.

TIME TO HIKE: optional, up to 5 days or more.

U.S.G.S. MAPS: Cedar Mesa, Grand Gulch and Goulding quadrangles.

HAZARDS: limited water; hazardous cliffs.

SEASONS: best from late spring through fall, but may be hiked in winter when snow is light.

ACCESS: drive south on Utah 261 from Utah 95 near turn-off to Natural Bridges National Monument, or drive northwest on Utah 261 from U.S. 163 north of Mexican Hat; Utah 261 roughly parallels rim of Johns Canyon as road travels southern end of Cedar Mesa; for access to Johns Canyon rim at mouth of main canyon, turn west off of Utah 261 near top of highway switchbacks that drop off of Cedar Mesa; at a road fork, turn right and continue to a canyon rim overlook that is just within Glen Canyon National Recreation Area; this overlook is at mouth of Johns Canyon; for access or egress farther up canyon rim, see Cedar Mesa topographic quadrangle for several points where rim and Utah 261 are ¼ to ½ mile apart.

TRAIL SUMMARY: Johns Canyon rim offers breathtaking views down into this lovely gorge, and hiking the wooded rim provides a good look at the rich vegetation and wildlife community of lofty Cedar Mesa.

TRAIL HIGHLIGHTS

Johns Canyon defines the slender southern tip of picturesque Cedar Mesa on the west. Thus, the western edge of that mesa is the eastern rim of Johns Canyon. Hiking that rim from the overlook at the southwestern tip of Cedar Mesa, to any of several points where the rim closely approaches Utah 261, will provide an excellent view of the picturesque canyon below, another mesa beyond and a close look at the pinyon-juniper forest that covers Cedar Mesa. This high plateau is bright with wildflowers of various sorts from late spring through fall, especially along the rimlands and in open meadows. Hikers with the time will find it worthwhile to descend from the rim into the canyon at any of many points in the upper canyon. There are Indian ruins in the upper arms of Johns Canyon. It is possible to hike on down the main canyon, where a rarely used off-road vehicle trail travels an intermediate level of the canyon below the high overlook and on out to Utah 261. Alternately, those with off-road vehicles might like to drive into Johns Canyon via this trail, then explore the upper canyon and rim on foot from a base camp in the upper canyon.

NOTES: It is possible to hike down the lower inner gorge of Johns Canyon to the San Juan River, but the last ¼ mile of this route is steep and hazardous. The off-road vehicle trail that enters Johns Canyon leaves Utah 261 about 6 miles southeast of the base of Cedar Mesa.

Lake Canyons

TYPE OF TRAILS: canyon-stream.

TRAIL MILEAGE: optional, up to 100 miles or more.

TIME TO HIKE: optional, up to several weeks.

U.S.G.S. MAPS: Browns Rim, Mt. Ellsworth, Mancos Mesa, The Rincon, Lake Canyon, Clay Hills, Navajo Mountain and No Mans Mesa quadrangles; a 1:250,000 scale topographic map of Lake Powell also covers these canyons, but in less detail.

HAZARDS: remote location; limited water in some canyons; canyons especially prone to flash flooding after rain on the adjacent highlands.

SEASONS: best during cooler months of spring or fall, but may be hiked in summer, or winter when snow is light.

ACCESS: even though a few remote backcountry off-road vehicle trails can be used for access to some of the canyons listed in this section, the only practical access and egress is via Lake Powell; for access to a specific canyon, use any map of the lake to reach the mouth of that canyon, boat as far up the canyon as practical, then hike on up the canyon bottom; for the lake access nearest these canyons, drive west on Utah 95 from U.S. 163, then southwest on Utah 263 from Utah 95; Halls Crossing Marina is at the end of Utah 263.

TRAIL SUMMARY: Hiking up some of the major tributary canyons that join Lake Powell between the Hite Marina and the San Juan arm of the lake provides access to some of the most remote and rarely seen desert-canyon country within the region covered by this book.

TRAIL HIGHLIGHTS

There are nine major canyons that branch from Lake Powell between its San Juan arm and Hite that are worth exploring. The lake penetrates each of these canyons for a distance, but each is also worth hiking on beyond the lake. They are, from the San Juan arm uplake, Cottonwood, Iceberg (or Wilson), Slickrock, Lake, Moki, Crystal Springs, Forgotten Knowles, and Cedar. Some of these are well-watered by flowing streams, others have intermittent or seasonal flow. Some are largely dry except following rain or spring thaws. Some have cottonwoods or other trees along their wash bottoms, and each is picturesque in its own way. Some were used as access routes to the Colorado River by the Anasazis, such as Forgotten and Iceberg. Several, such as Forgotten, Moki, Lake and Iceberg, had Anasazi settlements, but many of these prehistoric ruins are now drowned by Lake Powell. Cottonwood retains its identity as a canyon for only a couple of miles beyond the high water level, but it is interesting in that the Mormon pioneers who crossed the Colorado River below Hole in the Rock built a rock-terraced wagon trail out of the gorge, then con-

tinued up Cottonwood. The rock-terraces and Register Rock, where some of the pioneers scratched names and dates in a slickrock wall at the top of the grade, are now under water, but the old Mormon trail that remains is still followed on occasion by small groups of adventurous off-road vehicle enthusiasts. Iceberg or Wilson Canyon also retains its deep-canyon identity for only 2 miles or so beyond the lake, but is quite verdant and gives access to higher ground. Slickrock canyon is not penetrated as far by lake water as Iceberg, but is similar beyond the water's end. Lake Canyon has water in it for miles, and goes on for 5 or 6 miles beyond the end of the lake water. The canyon was named after Lake Pagahrit, a natural but highly unusual lake ½ mile long and ¼ mile wide that formed in prehistoric times when a tremendous flash flood down one arm of the canyon plugged another arm with rocks and debris more than 100 feet deep. The lake that resulted was used for hundreds of years by prehistoric and historic Indian tribes. The lake's name is Paiute for "standing water." The

Anasazis settled the lake area and the canyon below it quite heavily. The first white men to see the odd lake were the Mormon pioneers who came out of the Colorado River gorge by way of Cottonwood Canyon in 1879. Another heavy run-off overflowed the natural dam, cut it deeply and drained the strange lake in 1916. Moki Canyon is quite long. Lake Powell penetrates the picturesque slickrock canyon for several miles, then three main branches continue. It is about 11 miles to the end of the North Gulch branch. The two main branches of Moki continue for 15 and 20 miles, through spectacular canyons. Crystal Springs continues for 3 or 4 miles beyond the lake. Forgotten Canyon has two major forks, with lake water up each. One fork continues as a canyon for 3 or 4 miles beyond the lake water. The other is a mile or so longer. The Cedar Canyon system is probably the largest of the group. It is deep and narrow for a mile or so beyond the lake, then broadens for 2 or 3 miles and forks twice. The north fork is short. The southern two branches go on as deep and spectacular canyons for 10 and 12 miles, offering backpackers some really remote canyon wilderness.

NOTES: Some of the topographic maps of this area are too old to show Lake Powell and its high level up side-canyons. The vast highland drained by these canyon systems is largely Navajo sandstone slickrock, with a few patches of dark red Carmel mudstone and vast areas of living or stabilized sand dunes. This essentially solid rock surface permits rapid run-off from rain, and magnifies flash-flood danger in these canyons.

Extinct

Our little boat idled up a narrow, sheer-walled side-canyon a mile or so from the main body of Lake Powell. We were enjoying the ever-changing double image of canyon-and-reflection in the mirror-calm water ahead, and the soaring cliffs that loomed high above us.

The sandstone walls of the gorge were patterned with lichen streaks and desert varnish, with the patient sculptings of wind and water, and with the curving lines of ancient stress. Both walls were banded just above the water line with a narrow, seasonal belt of white left by the receding lake. The subdued, bubbling mutter of our boat's motor and our hushed voices echoed from the close canyon walls. We could hear the faint piping of a canyon wren in the distance.

As we rounded another bend, the canyon widened and a spring-seep alcove still high above the water caught our attention. The well-preserved ruins of a small group of Anasazi Indian dwellings occupied the deep alcove below a steeply sloping roof of raw sandstone only lightly streaked with brownish rain-runs from above. An odd pictograph done in white paint stood out on the wall above one dwelling.

My wife eyed the series of "Moki steps" and narrow ledges that gave access to the ancient dwellings from below. It was obvious what she had in mind. Had the canyon not been flooded, had a fall meant certain injury or worse on a rocky canyon floor, I would have flatly refused. As it was, why stifle an adventurous spirit with excessive caution?

I inched the boat over to the cliff face and up she went, fingers and deck shoes seeking notches and steps cut centuries ago by a people now extinct, for reasons still unclear to archeologists. As she climbed—ten, twenty, fifty feet upward—her busy eyes searched ahead and up, carefully, easily planning where each hand or foot would go next. Nothing to it!

I watched from the boat, which I had pulled away from the cliff and out of the way of a chance fall. I knew the worst was yet to come.

Fifteen minutes later, that time came. The first few yards of her descent were easy. The slope was not quite vertical, there were ledges a foot or so wide and she could see the next step or notch down. Then came the last forty feet or so of nearly perpendicular cliff.

Her progress slowed, and growing anxiety showed in every line and motion of her straining body. She looked repeatedly down at the dark, deep water seemingly so far below, then hung for long moments, motionless, her nose against the rough sandstone, forcing her pulse and breathing to slow their mad, fear-inspired pace.

She was scared silly! But fully aware that there was only one safe way to get down. From that height, impact with the water would be hard enough to injure, and subjectively it seemed ever farther down than it actually was.

I inched the boat closer, but still not below her, and talked calmly about the problem as she clung tightly to the cliff face. She responded in a tight voice barely short of panic.

"I'll talk you down. Just listen carefully and do exactly what I say." She agreed, encouraged by my matter-of-fact approach.

"Lower your left foot—a little more—now left six inches—there! Now get a lower grip with your right hand—you can see where to put it. Now, there's a little ledge directly below your right foot—farther yet. That's it!"

And so it went, step-by-step, inch-by-inch down the centuries-old Moki steps—steps that were traveled daily, often many times, by those who built them, and for yet another hundred feet of vertical distance that was now beneath water, down to the stream-watered canyon where crops then grew. Steps that in some Anasazi cliff-dwellings were sequenced so that you either knew the combination, or were stranded in an awkward position halfway up—with a long, fatal fall below.

Strangers not welcome!

When she had gotten down to about ten feet above the water, I told my exhausted wife to push out hard and drop into the water. After a few fearful looks downward, she did just that, entering the water feet first with a gurgling splash.

After she had climbed into the boat, grinning with relief, I said, more or less seriously—"You know, when the Anasazis lived here, there was no lake to cushion a fall from such steps. Do you suppose that's why they went extinct—just too many slipped getting up and down their tricky cliff-dwelling stairways?"

My soggy wife laughed—then gazed back up the cliff she had just come down, and looked very thoughtful.

172

Literature Useful in the Field

U.S. GEOLOGICAL SURVEY
Topographic quadrants, 1:62,500 series
Topographic map of Arches National Park
Topographic map of Canyonlands National Park

STATE
Utah State Travel Council Multipurpose Maps, #1 and #2. Obtain
   through local visitor centers or retail sales outlets.
Official Utah State Highway Map, widely distributed throughout the
   state, no charge.

OTHER
O. J. Murie, *A Field Guide to Animal Tracks,*" Houghton Mifflin Company
   pany
S. L. Welsh, *Flowers of the Canyon Country,* Brigham Young University
   sity Press
F. E. Mutschler, *Canyons of the Green & Colorado Rivers,* Volume II,
   Labyrinth, Stillwater & Cataract Canyons, Powell Society Ltd.
Brown, Yocum & Starbuck, *Wildlife of the Intermountain West,*
   Naturegraph Publishers.

Suggested Reading

D. L. Baars, *Redrock Country,* Doubleday & Co., Garden City, New
   York
D. G. Pike, *Anasazi,* American West Publishing Co., Palo Alto, California
   nia
C. G. Crampton, *Standing Up Country,* Knopf, New York, N.Y.
C. S. Peterson, *Look to the Mountains,* Brigham Young University
   Press, Provo, Utah
Edward Abbey & Philip Hyde, *Slickrock* Sierra Club, San Francisco,
   California & New York, N.Y.
David Muench & Hartt Wixom, *Utah* C. H. Belding, Portland, Oregon
Al Look, *1000 Million Years on the Colorado Plateau,* Bell Publications,
   Denver, Colorado
Faun McConkie Tanner, *The Far Country,* Olympus Publishing Company
   pany, Salt Lake City, Utah.

Photographs

OTHER WASATCH PUBLICATIONS

Canyon Country series

Wasatch Publishers maps and guidebooks can be purchased from retail outlets throughout canyon country or ordered directly from the publisher by mail for the prices listed, postpaid.

Wasatch Publishers, Inc.
4647 Idlewild Road
Salt Lake City, UT 84117

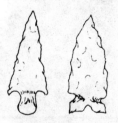